Working Women:
A Study of Women in Paid Jobs

Other Titles of Interest

The Underside of History: A View of Women Through Time,
Elise Boulding

Women in Changing Japan, edited by Joyce Lebra, Joy
Paulson, and Elizabeth Powers

*Women in Rural Development: A Survey of the Roles of
Women in Ghana, Lesotho, Kenya, Nigeria, Bolivia, Paraguay,
and Peru,* Donald R. Mickelwait, Mary Ann Riegelman, and
Charles F. Sweet

Covert Discrimination and Women in the Sciences, edited by
Judith A. Ramaley

*The Liberated Female: Life, Work, and Sex in Socialist
Hungary,* Ivan Volgyes and Nancy Volgyes

Westview Special Studies on Women in Contemporary Society

Working Women: A Study of Women in Paid Jobs
edited by Ann Seidman

The wages of women workers dropped from 63 to 57 percent of men's wages during the period from the 1950s to the 1970s. The unemployment rate for women wage earners is higher than that for men. Families headed by women constitute about one out of every three families with incomes below the poverty line. Minority women wage earners confront even greater problems than other women. All this remains true despite the passage of national and state legislation intended to provide equal employment opportunities and equal pay for equal work.

This book describes a regional pilot project that was organized to overcome the obstacles to women's advancement in the world of paid work. Almost one hundred women participated in the project. They were selected for their personal experience and knowledge of the problems women confront in seeking paid employment in blue collar, clerical, service, professional, or management/administrative fields. The book contains background information gathered in the course of the project, along with the participants' conclusions as to specific action programs and strategies that might be implemented to overcome barriers to the hiring and upgrading of women workers. It includes a selected annotated bibliography with about one hundred entries related to the special obstacles confronted by women wage earners in each major job category.

Ann Seidman is visiting professor of economics at the University of Massachusetts and visiting affiliate professor in Clark University's International Studies Program. Dr. Seidman served as project director for the Project on Expanding Career Options for Women at the Center for Research on Women, Wellesley College.

Working Women:
A Study of Women in Paid Jobs

---

edited by Ann Seidman

Contributors

Ramona Edelin
Roslyn Feldberg
Evelyn Nakano Glenn
Hilda Kahne
Doris Mitchell
Patricia Mittenthal
Irene Murphy
Brigid O'Farrell
Dorothy Parrish
Carol Ryser
Ann Seidman
Joan Wofford

Westview Press / Boulder, Colorado

Westview Special Studies on
Women in Contemporary Society

Copyright © 1978 by Westview Press, Inc.

Published in 1978 in the United States of America by
    Westview Press, Inc.
    5500 Central Avenue
    Boulder, Colorado 80301
    Frederick A. Praeger, Publisher

Library of Congress Cataloging in Publication Data
Main entry under title:
Working women.
    (Westview special studies on women in contemporary society)
    Bibliography: p.
    Includes index.
    1. Women—Employment—New England. I. Seidman, Ann. II. Edelin, Ramona.
HD 6096.A11W67   331.4'0974   77-13074
ISBN 0-89158-051-4

Printed and bound in the United States of America

Contents

Tables

Figures

Acknowledgments

This book describes a project that involved almost one hundred people in a collective process of formulation for effective action programs to improve the job opportunities and incomes of wage earning women. Twelve of these people, listed as contributors on the title page, met every other week for many months to prepare background materials, direct the intensive weekend workshops that formed the heart of the participatory process, and evaluate the results.

In the course of their work together, these twelve women produced a unified study that spoke for all. That is not to say that they never disagreed or argued (sometimes vehemently!), but through their debates and discussions the material incorporated into this book merged until it became difficult to precisely identify where the work of one person ended and the next began. All deserve credit for the vital role they played in the collective process.

The project organizers wish to express their sincere appreciation for the concerned participation of the women and men whose ideas made the workshops worthwhile. We would also like to express particular thanks to Judy Morse, executive secretary for the project, without whom it could never have been completed; to Judy Paquette and Margo Huntington and the work-study students (Pamela Burleson, Deidra Dixon, Mary Greene, and Terry Roemer) who assisted them; to the research assistants (Marianne Ajenian, Helen Goldman, Diane

Hurley, Debra Attiya Melton, Julianne Malveaux, Irma Claxton Scruggs, and Erline Willis) who aided the conveners in preparing these materials; to Dianne Painter for her willing assistance and for her specific contributions to some of the economic background materials; to Mary Jane Smalley, project officer of the Office of Education/HEW, who provided much-needed guidance at critical points; and to Carolyn Elliott, director of the Center for Research on Women at Wellesley, who offered invaluable constructive criticism and moral support for the project and for the preparation of this book.

About the Contributors

Ramona Edelin, formerly chairperson of the Department of Afro-American Studies of Northeastern University, is an Afro-American cultural analyst with a specialty in philosophy. In addition to teaching, she acts as a consultant on curriculum and program planning, language, culture, and media research. She is now working with the National Urban Coalition in Washington, D.C.

Roslyn L. Feldberg, an assistant professor of sociology at Boston University and a member of the Women's Research Center of Boston, has conducted research and written extensively about single parent families and clerical workers.

Evelyn Nakano Glenn, an assistant professor of sociology at Boston University, is interested in issues of women and work. She is currently carrying on research and writing about clerical workers and Asian-American women.

Hilda Kahne, a labor economist, is a professor of economics at Wheaton College. In 1975-76, she served as a consultant in policy research to the Wellesley Center for Research on Women. Her research and writing relate to women and the economy, career patterns, and job satisfaction.

Doris Mitchell is vice president for human resource management at Abt Associates where she deals with personnel and management planning. Formerly, she was associate dean of residence and assistant dean of students at Radcliffe College.

Patricia Hunter Mittenthal, a writer and a feminist, has

written a comprehensive guide to health care for women and helped to found the Women's Center of Hartford, Connecticut. Earlier she was a member of the Presidential Task Force on the War Against Poverty and a coordinator for the VISTA office and minority groups in California.

Irene L. Murphy, associate director of the project, is a policy analyst whose primary areas of interest are equal opportunity legislation and water resource conservation. After serving as executive director of the Federation of Organizations for Professional Women (1974-76), she joined the Carter-Mondale transition staff. Presently she is a senior consultant on water resource projects at the Department of Interior, Washington, D.C.

Brigid O'Farrell, research associate at the Center for Research on Women at Wellesley College, has designed and implemented research studies and action programs to aid in the successful integration of women into traditionally male occupations, specifically in blue collar craft and foremen jobs, working with private industry and unions.

Dorothy Parrish, social worker and community activist, has long been concerned with upgrading the status of service workers, primarily household workers. Formerly the research director of the Massachusetts Commission Against Discrimination, she is now a consultant and member of the boards of directors of several community organizations, including the National Committee on Household Employment, the Boston YWCA, and Winners (Women's Innercity Resource Center).

Carol Ryser, sociologist, has worked as consultant, teacher, and researcher on projects concerning the psychology and sociology of women. She is especially concerned with the action implications of research on these issues.

Ann Seidman, project director, one of the authors, and editor of this book, is an economist and a visiting professor at the University of Massachusetts–Amherst and Clark University. She is a member of the Massachusetts Governor's Commission on the Status of Women, and previously taught and conducted research for eight years in African universities, in addition to working in several universities in the United States.

Joan Wofford, an educational consultant, is a partner in Leadership and Learning, Inc., chairperson of the Lincoln-Sudbury Regional School Committee, and currently preparing a book with two colleagues on the management of decline in the school system.

1

Why a Pilot Project?

Low Pay, High Rates of Unemployment

Almost one out of two women in the United States works for pay. But women earn wages that are little more than half those of men. Despite the passage of laws and administrative rulings providing equal pay for equal work, the median wage for women, overall, actually declined from 63 percent of the median wage for men in the 1950s to 57 percent in the 1970s.[1]

More and more women have entered the paid labor force in recent years, far exceeding expectations based on past trends. From 1947 to 1965, the proportion of women in paid jobs increased from 32 to 39 percent of all adult women. In the next decade alone, this proportion rose by as much as in the preceding 18 years, to 46 percent. Today, about half of all adult women hold paid jobs.

This accelerating increase in the number of women wage earners may reflect, in part, the impact of inflation and unemployment among men. More and more women have had to take paid jobs to help support their families.

Patterns of family life, too, have changed. More women have fewer children so they may return to the paid labor force and remain in it for longer periods of time than in bygone years. One out of every three marriages ends in divorce, leaving more women with the primary responsibility for supporting their families.

While more women seek to enter paid employment, higher proportions of women than men suffer from unemploy-

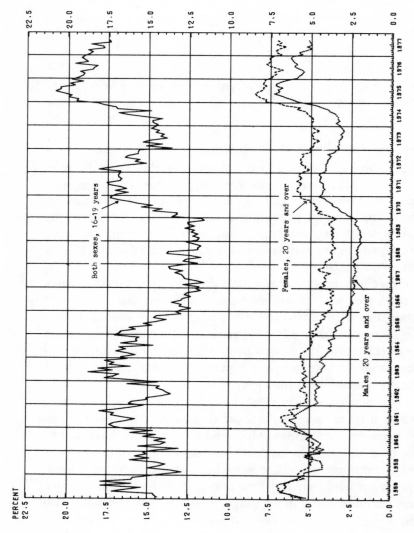

Figure 1.1 Unemployment rates by sex and age, U.S. (seasonally adjusted). Source: U.S., Department of Labor, Bureau of Labor Statistics, *Employment and Earnings* (Washington, D.C., Government Printing Office, 1977), vol. 24, no. 1, p. 13.

ment (Fig. 1.1). Men were more seriously affected by the recession of the mid-1970s than women, primarily because women are segregated into different kinds of jobs than men. Traditional male jobs, especially construction work and basic industries, were, as Fig. 1.2 indicates, harder hit by unemployment than clerical and service industries, in which more women are employed. On the other hand, within the blue collar category, operative jobs, in which most women blue collar workers are employed, were more severely affected than the predominantly male skilled crafts jobs. The professional, management, and administrative categories, where men predominate, were least affected by unemployment, although even there unemployment emerged as a major problem in 1975 and 1976. Under the impact of all these factors combined, unemployment rates among women continued to exceed those among men, although the gap tended to narrow in the recession of the 1970s.

Critics of national unemployment data point out that official statistics exclude many discouraged workers who have given up the active search for jobs. This may have been a significant factor in the decline in labor force participation rates of men in 1975-6 (Fig. 1.3). Furthermore, part-time workers who might have preferred full-time jobs had they been available, are also excluded from official data. Both categories include a large number of women, although the increase of women entering the labor force tends to obscure the fact that other women may have become discouraged and dropped out.

The Urban League, taking into account discouraged and part-time workers, estimated[2] overall unemployment nationally to be 15.6 percent in April-June 1975, almost double the U.S. Department of Labor figure of 8.9 percent. The league estimated unemployment among blacks and other minorities to be 26.1 percent, compared to the Labor department's 14.3 percent.[3]

Many programs have been mounted in recent years in an effort to uncover and eliminate factors that contribute to lower incomes and greater rates of unemployment for women. These programs range from projects that assist indi-

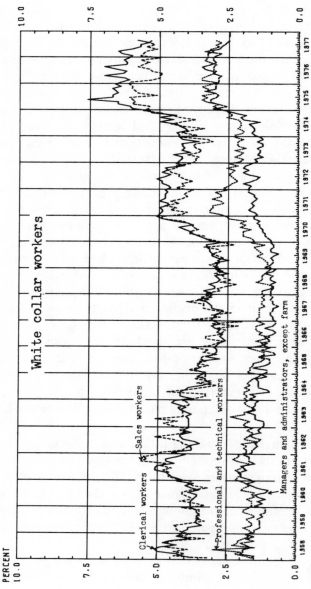

Figure 1.2 Unemployment rates by major occupational groups, U.S. (seasonally adjusted). Source: U.S., Department of Labor, Bureau of Labor Statistics, *Employment and Earnings* (Washington, D.C., Government Printing Office, 1977), vol. 24, no. 1, p. 18.

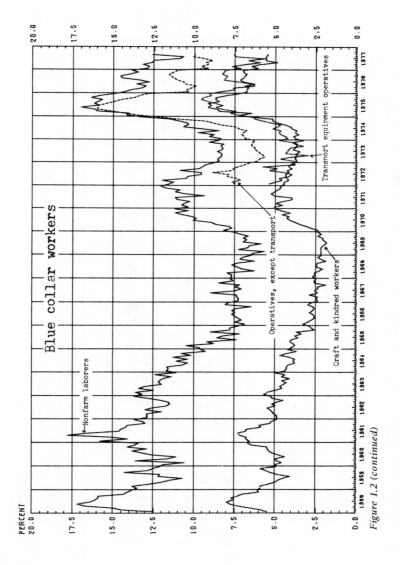

Figure 1.2 (continued)

6

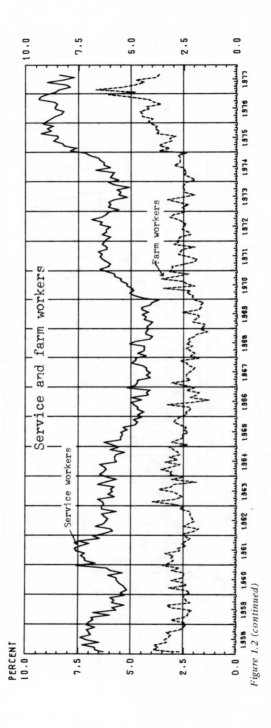

Figure 1.2 (continued)

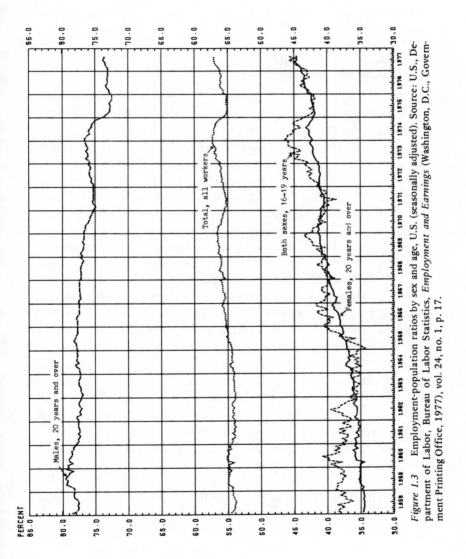

Figure 1.3 Employment-population ratios by sex and age, U.S. (seasonally adjusted). Source: U.S., Department of Labor, Bureau of Labor Statistics, *Employment and Earnings* (Washington, D.C., Government Printing Office, 1977), vol. 24, no. 1, p. 17.

vidual women to acquire improved work skills to legislation
designed to guarantee equal employment opportunities and
pay. But the problems persist. The questions arise: Why have
existing programs had so little real impact? How can they be
improved?

A Pilot Project To Expand
the Career Options of Women

In 1975, the Center for Research on Women at Wellesley
College received a one-year contract from the Office of Education of the Department of Health, Education, and Welfare[4]
to conduct a pilot participatory project to find more effective ways to alter the constraints that narrow the career options of women throughout the nation. The underlying
premise of the project was that those constraints have
become institutionalized, imbedded in the particular sets of
practices and institutions that have emerged in the course of
the history of each region to shape women's job opportunities. The aim was to escape from generalized overall explanations of the problems ("what everybody knows") and to involve women who themselves work for pay in identifying the
ways particular regional institutions and practices restrict
their job options and in formulating more effective programs
to change them.

Women, along with minorities in the United States and
peoples in the Third World, are increasingly demanding that
they be involved in research concerning the pressing issues
that affect their lives.[5] The pilot project was built around a
problem-solving approach to make this possible.

The problem-solving approach incorporates five basic
steps.

1. The identification and definition of the problems to be
   solved.
2. The explicit formulation of the range of explanations
   as to how objective conditions cause the problems.
3. Testing the explanations to determine which are valid
   in the sense that they are consistent with available evidence.

4. Formulation of proposals for solution, that is, strategies and action programs directed to overcoming the causes of the problems identified by the validated explanations.
5. Evaluation of the consequences of implementing the proposed programs and strategies. (This commonly leads to the identification of new problems, hopefully on a higher level, which may then be tackled by using the same methodology.)

The Wellesley project sought to enable women wage earners, with knowledge of a localized labor market born of their personal experience, to participate in identifying the problems they confront, critically examining the alternative explanations commonly proposed, and formulating more effective action programs and strategies to improve women's job opportunities.

This kind of process could not meaningfully be conducted for the entire United States at the same time. It was decided, therefore, to focus on a pilot study of one region which might then be replicated in other parts of the nation.[6]

New England is a useful region for this kind of pilot study. It includes a major mature industrialized area, one of the oldest in the nation, centered around eastern Massachusetts, Rhode Island, and Connecticut. The much larger areas of Maine, New Hampshire, and Vermont (see Fig. 1.4) are relatively less industrialized.

Analysis of the conditions shaping women's work in New England provides valuable insights into trends that may emerge in other regions as they become increasingly industrialized.

As a mature industrial economy, New England differs in several ways from other regions of the nation. It is primarily an industrial state, importing food and other agricultural produce from areas more suitable for large-scale farming. As a result, a far smaller proportion of the paid labor force in New England is employed on farms than in southern and western states. A slightly higher proportion of women work for pay in New England than nationally. Since less than 5 percent of

Figure 1.4 Women wage earners in New England in 1970. Source: U.S., Department of Commerce, *Census of Population, 1970* (Washington, D.C., Government Printing Office, 1970), "Characteristics of Population (by state)," Table 54.

all wage earning women in New England work on farms, this category of employment was excluded from the pilot project.[7]

In New England, a higher proportion of women than men work in blue collar jobs than in states like Missouri, California, Michigan, and Ohio.[8] A higher proportion of New England women have also entered clerical and professional employment as these categories have expanded in recent years. A smaller proportion of women, compared to men, on the other hand, work in service jobs in New England than in states like Florida, South Carolina, and Washington. This may be, in part, because in the latter states, regional discriminatory practices restrict women's opportunities in other fields, leaving service jobs as the main kind women may obtain.

Compared to New England, many more black and other minority workers are concentrated in low-paying service, farm, and blue collar work, not only in the southern states, but also in Illinois, Michigan, California, and New York. In the South, this may be a carryover of institutionalized racist attitudes and practices from the slavery era. The blacks, who migrated north during the war and postwar periods, tended in the first instance to move to the major industrial states of the East and Midwest. Only in more recent years have they moved beyond to the older New England industrial areas.

The wages of women workers vary significantly within and between the regions of the nation. The median wages of men and women in Massachusetts, for example, are significantly higher than those in Western agrarian states like Wyoming, as well as those in the less industrialized northern tier states of New England itself: Vermont, New Hampshire, and Maine. On the other hand, in Massachusetts, women's wages are lower than women's wages in the industrial state of Illinois, while men in Massachusetts earn more than men in Illinois.

Careful analysis of these kinds of differences in the patterns of employment and wages between regions may help to explain the way institutionalized attitudes and practices interact with the differing characteristics of the regional labor market to shape the options of women seeking paid jobs. The

Wellesley project, by concentrating on the way these factors operate in the New England context, was designed to help build up this essential fund of knowledge.

The Organization of the Project

The project was divided into three phases. Phase I consisted of a literature search and preparation of background materials and bibliographies related to each of the major employment categories. This phase, which lasted two months, was conducted by an interdisciplinary team of workshop conveners. Each convener was, herself,[9] an expert in the employment area for which she was responsible. Each prepared a booklet that identified the main obstacles to better employment and income opportunities for women in her particular job category and outlined the major explanations and possible solutions suggested in the literature. The conveners met biweekly as a group to discuss, criticize, and revise these booklets.

Phase II consisted of a series of eight weekend workshops involving carefully selected participants, most of whom were employed in the relevant job categories. The workshops constituted the heart of the project. There, the participants brought together knowledge from their rich and widely varied experiences to search for more effective action. The first workshop dealt with difficulties that confront all women seeking paid jobs, such as employment counseling, adequate child care, and transportation facilities. The second focused on special additional barriers that confront black and other minority women in the paid labor market. The next five workshops dealt with the barriers women face in the major employment categories defined by the United States census: blue collar, including factory operatives, craftsmen, and laborers; clerical;[10] service, including health, food, and household workers; professions, including teachers, medical and legal personnel, and researchers of all kinds; and management and administration. The final workshop was devoted to designing and illustrating the use of a model for implementing strategies to change educational and other institutions to improve women's career options.

Each workshop was deliberately kept quite small. This made it possible to explore in depth the key issues in a weekend of intense discussion and debate. The participants were carefully selected because of their knowledge of the category of employment under consideration. A high proportion of the women were "representative" of the employees of the given category as a result of their own work experiences. They were chosen for their known ability to analyze the causes and possible solutions to the problems they and their coworkers confront in the specific institutional setting of New England. Some are policy makers—persons engaged in the formulation and/or implementation of legislative and administrative rulings relating to women wage earners. A resource person, who had conducted extensive research relating to relevant issues, was included in each workshop. Employer representatives were invited, but, for the most part, they preferred to make only short presentations, rather than to remain for the give-and-take of the full two days.

Table 1.1 shows the numbers of participants who took part from each of the three major categories. Some of the participants were counted in two categories so the total number exceeds the actual number who took part.

Statistics cannot, however, capture the depths of experience or vibrant enthusiasm that the participants brought to the workshops. A young mother of five, living in a Boston suburb, described her initial chagrin at having to use food stamps to feed her children after her husband's business went bankrupt, and until she could find a job. A divorced mother of three told of her efforts to organize welfare mothers to improve their lot in rural New Hampshire. A black dean of a women's college explained how she had struggled to obtain an education after beginning life as a migrant worker on a tobacco farm in the Connecticut River Valley. A Portuguese woman, who rejected her family's pleas to marry and settle down, developed a career organizing unions among Portuguese-speaking women in the New Bedford textile mills. A Native American grandmother, herself a mother of ten, described her realization of the way welfare, instead of paid employment, had sapped the self-reliance of her people on

Table 1.1

Participants in Eight New England Workshops on Working Women *

I. Researchers	9
II. Representatives	
A. Organized groups	
1. Occupational status	
a. professional	4
b. labor unions	6
c. clerical	4
d. other	5
2. Service	
a. health	3
b. employment counseling	12
c. other	2
3. Research and educational institutions	12
4. Political action groups	2
B. Educational institutions	8
C. Business, industry	10
III. Policy Makers	
A. Federal level administrators	7
B. State level administrators and legislators	14
C. Local level administrators	4

* Some of the participants are represented in more than one category, so the total adds up to a greater number than the number of persons who actually participated in the workshops.

the Penobscott Reservation in Maine; at fifty, she had gone to college to acquire the skills needed to help improve their life options. A distinguished chemist from Rhode Island reported on her work of building an employment network to enable professional women to find careers commensurate with their capabilities. A black elementary school principal, formerly a Marine colonel, described a program in which role models (women computer programmers, doctors, mechanics, lawyers) were brought to his biracial school in a chronically depressed area to give the pupils a broader perspective as to their possible career choices. A labor educator told of her program to teach blue collar women how to participate more effectively in the collective bargaining process.

In Phase III of the project, the conveners worked together to compile and record the recommendations of the workshops, to prepare materials for dissemination, and to plan how they might best be distributed to encourage similar undertakings elsewhere in the nation. This book is a product of their work.

The book is divided into four parts. The first part examines the New England economy and public policies as they affect women wage earners in the area. It suggests some of the major similarities and differences between New England and other regions of the nation. The second part lays out the evidence of the barriers confronting all women seeking paid jobs in New England. The third part examines the particular features of the institutions and practices that hinder the entry and upgrading of women in five major employment categories: clerical, service, blue collar, professional, and management and administration. The fourth part summarizes the action programs and strategies proposed by the workshop participants.

It is hoped that, by critically comparing the circumstances that define women's career options in New England with those prevailing elsewhere, the readers will be able to draw on the proposals made by the workshop participants to formulate more effective programs to broaden women's paid employment opportunities in their own regions.

Part 1
Economic and Political Background

2
New England's Mature Industrial Economy

Where Women Work for Pay in New England

New England is the oldest industrial region in the nation. This is reflected in the changes in the structure of employment that have taken place there since World War II. Between 1947 and 1973, regional employment grew from 3.3 million to 4.7 million jobs, an increase of 41 percent. This is much less than the 72 percent growth in national employment during the same period. The importance of manufacturing industries has declined in New England, while service and clerical industries have expanded rapidly.

As the structure of employment has changed, more women have entered paid jobs in New England. The 1970 census[1] reported that about 4.8 million adult women, 16 years and older, lived in New England. Of these, 2.2 million had paying jobs. Slightly more women, proportionately, worked for pay in New England than nationally (46 compared to 44 percent). A much higher proportion of black and other minority women, 53 percent, were in the paid labor force in New England as well as throughout the country.

Since 1970, the national average of women in the paid labor market has risen to over 49 percent, exceeding the 1970 New England level. Unfortunately, until the 1980 census results are available, it will not be known whether New England's female labor force participation still exceeds the national average.[2] The data from the 1980 census may show an even higher rate of employment among women in New England because of the higher regional rate of unem-

19

ployment among men.

By far the largest number of employed women and men in New England work in the major industrial areas in the more populous states of Massachusetts and Connecticut and in Providence, Rhode Island (see Fig. 2.1). Two out of three women wage workers are employed in five cities: Boston, Massachusetts; Providence, Rhode Island; and Hartford, New Haven, and Bridgeport, Connecticut. More than four out of five (83 percent) of all black and other minority workers are employed in those cities. Job opportunities for women are more limited in other New England areas, and median wages there are lower than in the five cities cited.

The growing employment of women wage workers over the last quarter of a century reflects, in part, the changing structure of the New England labor force. Some job categories have expanded, while others have contracted. Farm work has declined rapidly. In the South and West of the United States, in contrast, it would be essential to examine the employment status of women in farm work.

Nondurable consumer goods industries, like apparel and textiles, and durable goods industries, like electrical appliances, have long been important in New England. In recent decades, however, with new technological advances being introduced at a geometric rate, machines have replaced people in a wide range of industries. Also, former skilled crafts have been divided into an increasing number of simple, unskilled jobs. Women, often recent immigrants, tend to be hired for these jobs. The growing employment of women in this category has helped reduce labor costs. In Massachusetts, for example, the median wage for women operatives in 1970 was barely more than half that of men.

Despite the increase in less skilled factory jobs, the overall employment of both men and women in the blue collar category has been growing slowly in New England. It actually declined in Massachusetts, even before the recession of the mid-seventies. Earlier, New England lost manufacturing plants to the low wage areas of the South. More recently, many of the simplified assembly and processing jobs have been transferred to low-wage areas overseas. Big firms with major plants in New England, like General Electric, for example, have been expanding their operations in South Africa, where African workers, under conditions termed "slave labor" by the International Labor Organization, earn about one-sixth of the average American wage.

Another feature of the change in the structure of the New England labor force has been the expansion of the number of workers employed in the allocation of materials and supplies and the sale of goods on an ever-expanding scale by United States-based multinationals. This is reflected in the rapidly growing clerical and sales force. Here the number of women workers exceeds that of men throughout the region. The employment of low-paid women in these jobs helps to reduce labor costs. In Massachusetts, the major administrative and distributive center of New England, the median wage for a female clerical worker is about $4,762, compared to $6,789 for a male blue collar worker.

Service work has expanded rapidly as the structure of the economy and the labor force has shifted throughout New England. This category includes employment in cleaning, health, food, personal, protective, and private household work. Today, service work employs more women than men and closely rivals blue collar work as an employer of women. Minority women are most likely to be hired for service jobs, especially in private households.

Women in New England have found more job opportunities in the professional category over the past two decades. A large proportion of women in this category are teachers, mostly in the lower grades. Lower-level health opportunities have also been expanding for women. The opportunities for women in management and administration in New England, as throughout the nation, remain sharply restricted, although they have increased slightly in recent years. Women still constitute a far smaller percentage of all workers in this field than in the New England labor force as a whole.

The resulting profile of the female labor force in New England, like that in the nation, resembles a pyramid with by far the largest proportion of women employed in clerical, sales, and service jobs. Blue collar work, which used to be the pri-

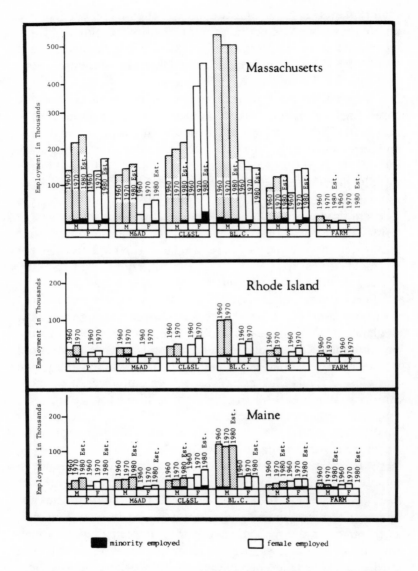

Figure 2.1 Growth of male and female employment by major categories, with estimates for 1980. The 1960 and 1970 data are taken from the census for those years. The 1980 figures are estimated by a straightline projection of the employment rates for men and women in each job category for 1970 in the context of overall employment estimates made by the Division of Employment Security in each state in cooperationwith the Bureau of Labor Statistics. This procedure is based on the (hopefully erroneous) assumption that there will be no change in

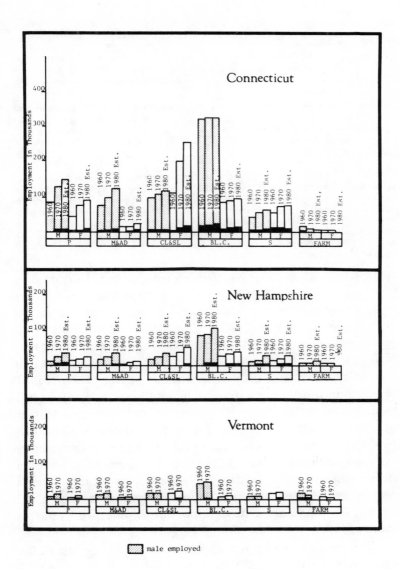

male employed

the proportions of women compared to men in any category from 1970 to 1980. Since the state projections available at the time of the project failed to take into account the impact of the 1970s recession, they are probably overestimated. Source: U.S., Department of Commerce, *Census of Population, 1970* (Washington, D.C., Government Printing Office, 1970), "Characteristics of Population (by state)," vol. 1, pt. 23, Tables 46, 122, 170.

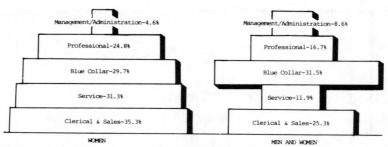

Figure 2.2   Profile of the female labor force compared to the total labor force in New England in 1970. (Percentages do not add up to 100.0 because farm workers and managers have been excluded.) About 35 percent of New England women professionals are elementary and secondary school teachers compared to about 17 percent of all professionals. Another 22 percent of New England women professionals are nurses. Source: U.S., Department of Commerce, *Census of Population, 1970* (Washington, D.C., Government Printing Office, 1970), "Characteristics of Population (by state)," Table 54.

mary sector of employment for women, is now in third place. The top of the pyramid consists of professional workers. Only a tiny percent reaches the peak management and administration posts (see Fig. 2.2). The profile of the labor force participation by men and women combined reflects the very different pattern of employment among men who make up almost two-thirds of all workers. A far higher proportion of men are in blue collar work and management and administration. A far smaller proportion of men are in clerical and sales or service work. The smaller proportion of men in these professions reflects two factors: (1) a far higher proportion of male professionals advance into the management/administration category, and (2) about 57 percent of women professionals are elementary and secondary school teachers and nurses, whereas only a tiny proportion of men are employed in these fields.

Women tend to be found in the lower paying, less skilled categories, regardless of their educational qualifications. As Table 2.1 illustrates, in Massachusetts, the most populous New England state, men are far more likely than women of the same educational background to become managers, administrators, or craftspersons. Women with college educations are more likely to be in clerical or service work. At the other end of the educational scale, women with less than

Table 2.1

Percentage Distribution of Men and Women in Massachusetts in Each Employment Category According to Number of School Years Completed, 1970

Percentage of Women and Men in each Employment Category According to Number of School Years Completed

	Percentage of Men and Women in Each Employment Category		8 Years or Less of Elementary School		High School				College			
					1-3 Years		4 Years		1-3 Years		4 Years	
	M	F	M	F	M	F	M	F	M	F	M	F
Professional	17.8	16.8	1.4	1.8	3.1	3.2	8.7	8.5	42.3	27.5	98.7	74.0
Management/Admin.	11.9	3.1	4.6	1.2	6.5	0.7	11.7	1.2	19.9	2.9	20.3	5.5
Sales	6.9	7.1	2.9	4.9	5.6	5.1	7.3	7.6	12.3	5.8	20.9	2.0
Clerical	8.6	36.6	4.5	6.6	8.6	21.1	11.3	51.9	14.2	47.7	4.2	14.1
Craftsperson	22.3	1.6	26.2	3.4	25.2	2.4	27.5	1.0	13.2	0.7	2.3	----
Operatives (except transport)	13.2	16.5	25.8	48.8	18.6	26.8	11.5	10.9	6.0	2.3	0.5	0.6
Laborers (except farm)	5.3	0.7	9.2	1.5	8.9	1.2	4.4	0.5	3.1	0.2	0.1	0.1
Service (except private household)	9.8	14.1	14.7	20.5	14.1	23.9	9.7	14.0	8.0	10.8	4.3	2.1
Private household	0.4	1.5	0.6	4.7	0.9	2.4	0.2	0.9	0.8	0.6	0.06	0.2
Totals	100.0	100.0	100.0	100.0	100.0	100.0	100.0	100.0	100.0	100.0	100.0	100.0

Source: Calculated from U. S., Department of Commerce, Census of the Population, 1970 (Washington, D.C., Government Printing Office, 1970), "Detailed Characteristics for Massachusetts," Table 179.

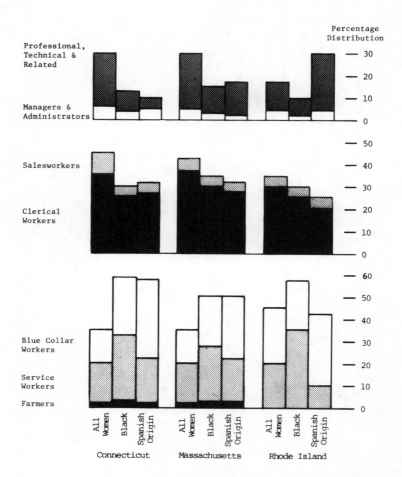

Figure 2.3   Where minority women work: occupational distribution, by percent, of all women, black women, and women of Spanish origin in the three most industrialized New England states in 1970. Source: Statistics from U.S., Department of Commerce, *Census of Population, 1970* (Washington, D.C., Government Printing Office, 1970), "Detailed characteristics (by state)," Table 54.

three years of high school are more likely than men in that group to be factory operatives. This is even more true for women compared to men who have eight years or less of elementary school.

Black, Hispanic, and other minority women tend to be employed in the least desirable lowest paying jobs (see Fig. 2.3). This is true even when they have the same educational qualifications as other women.

It is not infrequently argued that the reason women are not upgraded in accordance with their educational qualifications is because they are not dependable workers. They are said to be absent and to quit their jobs more often than men. Many studies show, however, that most women are dependable and committed to doing a good job in the world of paid work. Although some may leave their jobs when they have children, three-fourths do not. National studies show that the overall rate of turnover among women is slightly higher than among men, but even this difference tends to disappear when women, who are concentrated in low-paying, unattractive work categories, are compared with men doing the same kind of work. The same may be true, too, for absenteeism among women as compared to men, although more research is required in this area.

Low Wages

The median wage[3] of full-time women workers in New England is slightly higher than the national median wage relative to men's (58 percent compared to 57 percent). If part-time workers are included, the overall median wage of New England women workers is pulled way down to 47 percent of men's, slightly less than the national 48 percent. It has been estimated that four out of five women who work part time do so because they have no alternative. Therefore the lower figure is perhaps a more realistic indicator of the median wage most women are actually able to earn, given the job opportunities available to them. The median wage of black and other minority women is significantly less than that of all women.

Figure 2.4 compares women's wages to men's nationally in 1964 and 1974. Figure 2.5 illustrates the pattern of women's and men's wages in 1970 in Massachusetts, the New England state where the largest numbers of women work for pay. Women are concentrated at the low end of the income scale. The median wage of all women who worked for pay, including those working part time, in 1970, was $3,741, about half that considered essential by the United States

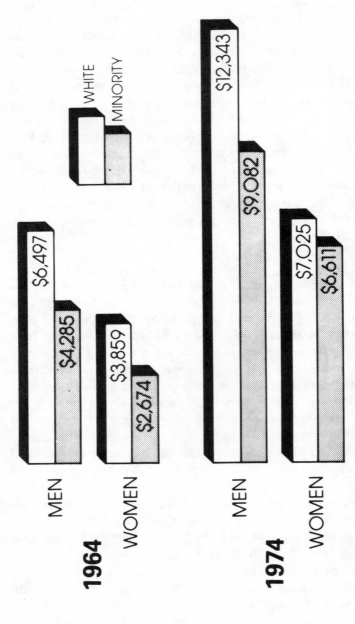

1964

MEN $6,497 — WHITE
$4,285 — MINORITY

WOMEN $3,859 — WHITE
$2,674 — MINORITY

1974

MEN $12,343 — WHITE
$9,082 — MINORITY

WOMEN $7,025 — WHITE
$6,611 — MINORITY

WHITE
MINORITY

Figure 2.4 Fully employed women continue to earn less than fully employed men of either white or minority races (minority includes all races other than white). Source: U.S., Department of Labor, Employment Standards Administration, Women's Bureau; data from U.S., Department of Commerce, Bureau of the Census.

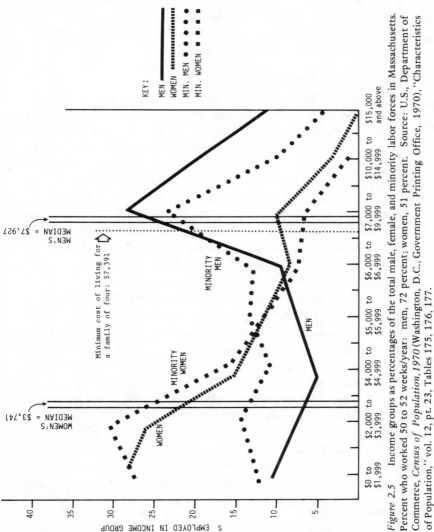

Figure 2.5 Income groups as percentages of the total male, female, and minority labor forces in Massachusetts. Percent who worked 50 to 52 weeks/year: men, 72 percent; women, 51 percent. Source: U.S., Department of Commerce, *Census of Population, 1970* (Washington, D.C., Government Printing Office, 1970), "Characteristics of Population," vol. 12, pt. 23, Tables 175, 176, 177.

Bureau of Labor Statistics to support a family of four at
what might be termed a minimum health and decency level.
The wages of almost half the men were also below that
figure. A significantly higher proportion of minority men
than all men earned wages below it. This would appear to be
important in explaining why so many women must work to
help support their families.

The Impact of Unemployment

There has been a serious problem of growing unemployment in New England since the late 1960s.[4] The expansion of
available jobs has not kept pace with the growing number of
men and women who have been seeking paid work. This
problem reached near-crisis proportions in the 1975 recession, with unemployment in Massachusetts 50 percent higher
than the national average. There the unemployment rate for
all workers was about 12 percent in April 1975 compared to
8 percent for the nation. The estimated unemployment rate
among white women was over 13 percent.[5] Among black and
minority women, the unemployment rate was over 20 percent, almost twice the average for all workers.

In some towns, like New Bedford, Massachusetts, where
industries were especially hard hit by the mid-1970s slump,
the overall rate of unemployment reached 16 percent. In
such areas, it was estimated that nearly one out of five
women and one out of four minority women who wanted to
work did not have paid jobs.

Younger and older women workers were more seriously
affected by unemployment than the average, both in New
England and throughout the nation. Unemployment is particularly acute for young minority women. In Boston, for
example, their estimated unemployment rate ran as high as
45 to 50 percent in 1975. Older minority women also confront particular difficulties in finding new jobs when they are
laid off.

Forecasters suggest that unemployment may be a long-
term feature of the national economy.[6] An estimated 5 to 8
percent unemployment rate may persist even after economic
"recovery" is said to have taken place. Such forecasts suggest

Table 2.2

Poverty Status of All Families and Families Headed by Women in New England
States, 1970 (Percentage with Incomes Below Poverty Level)

	Families with Income Below Poverty Level			Female-Headed Families with Income Below Poverty Level		
	White	Black	Spanish-American	White	Black	Spanish-American
Massachusetts	5.7	22.4	20.1	38.9	76.7	39.2
Connecticut	4.5	19.2	16.5	37.5	67.5	48.1
Maine	10.3	15.1	8.1	29.5	46.0	24.3
New Hampshire	7.1	(a)	4.0	23.6	23.6	(a)
Rhode Island	6.4	(a)	19.4	29.4	(a)	60.0
Vermont	9.2	(a)	2.0	20.9	(a)	(a)

Source: Calculated from U. S., Department of Commerce, Census of
Population, 1970 (Washington, D.C., Government Printing Office, 1970),
"Characteristics of Population (by State)", Table 58.

Note: [a]Insignificant percentage of families.

that, given New England's higher unemployment rate, some 7
to 11 percent of all workers may remain unemployed there in
the longer run.[7]

Poverty

In New England, as well as throughout the nation, families headed by women are far more likely to be poor than
those headed by men because of the low wages most women
can earn. Even before the mid-1970s recession, a significant
number of New England families lived below the poverty
line, the $3,743 estimated by the United States Bureau of
Labor statistics as the bare minimum necessary in 1970 to
sustain a family of four. A higher proportion of the population (7 to 10 percent) in the more rural northern tier states
lived below the poverty level than in Massachusetts (6 percent) or Connecticut (5 percent), reflecting the lower wages

paid in the more rural states. The absolute number of impoverished families living in the more industrialized states, is, however, much larger, since the total population is greater in those states.

About two out of five poor families in Massachusetts and Connecticut were headed by women in 1970. The proportion was slightly higher in New Hampshire and Maine. The situation is worse for black and other minority families, whose incomes are lower and unemployment greater (see Table 2.2).

Poverty restricts the life options, not only of these women, but also of their entire families. Their children are less likely than those of other families to enjoy adequate food, clothing, and shelter. They are much less likely to obtain the kinds of education required to broaden their future career options. As a result of the low incomes they are able to earn—even when they do find paid jobs—these women and their families are enmeshed in a vicious circle of poverty from which it is difficult to escape.

3
The Failure of Public Policy

In New England, women's rights to equal pay and job opportunities are provided, not only by national laws and administrative rulings, but also by more extensive state legislation than exists in many other regions. Nevertheless, public policy appears to have been unable, so far, to significantly improve the job status of women in the region.

Increased demand for equal opportunity for women wage earners since World War II has resulted in the formulation of national, state, and local policies that seek to bar discriminatory practices because of sex, race, religion, nationality, or age.[1] These policies and the consequences of efforts to implement them are reviewed briefly below in terms of their implications for the working conditions affecting women in New England at the time of the project. It should be emphasized that public policy is continually being changed, not only by legislative actions, but also by court interpretations, which may materially affect their scope and enforcement.

State Equal Employment Programs[2]

Fair Employment Practices Commissions

Today's legislation on equal employment and educational opportunity can be traced to the pressure for fairer treatment of minorities that began in the full-employment days of World War II. At that time, President Franklin D. Roosevelt signed two executive orders. The first created a small staff to develop greater employment opportunity for minorities.

The staff worked, ironically, in a federal building with a segregated cafeteria. A second order created the Fair Employment Practices Committee in the Executive Office. Congress abolished that committee in 1946, leaving the states to decide whether to adopt its all too briefly tested model.

By 1949, a half-dozen states and some cities (notably Detroit and New York where militant and occasionally violent demands had been expressed for fairer treatment for blacks) had established commissions to promote equal job opportunities. By 1966, twenty-eight states had administrative agencies with authority to handle complaints of job discrimination against minorities. These agencies often have jurisdiction over discriminatory practices relating to age, housing, and credit, as well as employment. Sex discrimination was declared an illegal practice in the sixties.[3] State commissions, now operating in nearly every state, use similar procedures to achieve similar goals. An individual complaint of discrimination leads to an investigation to establish whether there has been "probable" cause for state intervention to end a discriminatory practice. If probable cause is found, a settlement is sought. If there is no settlement, a hearing is held. The agency, or, if it lacks authority, a court then orders the cessation of the discriminatory practice. State commissions have not initiated complaints themselves. Instead, commission investigators respond to cases brought forward by complainants. Limited staff and funding cause severe delays in processing each case. This not only hinders the cause of justice for the woman or minority person who must continue to work in situations they believe to be unfair. It also demoralizes others who consider themselves aggrieved, but see no advantage in filing complaints.

A review of the records of several state commissions by Duane Lockard[4] cites many obstacles to effective implementation of fair employment practices on the state level. Governors and legislators have failed to support authority and/or funding for the state agencies. The experience of the Commission Against Discrimination in Massachusetts, one of the earliest established, illustrates the problems. Even prior to 1975, the Massachusetts commission was criticized, in addition to other reasons, because its commissioners served only part time. It was already accumulating an increasing backlog of complaints. In 1975, in company with many such agencies in other states, the Massachusetts commission was caught in the economic crunch. Its budget was slashed by about one-third, although demands for its services were rising. Many staff members were laid off and three branch offices were closed. Since the branch offices handled a variety of complaints for persons who could not travel to Boston, their closure was especially serious. The state secretary of administration and finance, who is responsible for the Massachusetts commission, declared that it might as well be totally abolished.

> At its present level of funding, the MCAD can handle only the tip of the iceberg in dealing with unlawful discrimination. Although its work is of the utmost concern and importance, its relatively high cost-service ratio raises the question of whether the state can afford to continue its existence.[5]

In 1977, however, three full-time commissioners were appointed. The budget remains small, but this appeared to be a helpful step in the right direction.

Other Types of State Legislation

Four kinds of laws have been passed by various states relating to equal employment opportunities. Of the six New England states, only Massachusetts has enacted all four. They include measures[6] that are similar to federal policies.

1. Equal pay laws, similar to the National Equal Pay Act.
2. State contract laws, like the federal executive orders that established the Office of Federal Contract Compliance Programs, to outlaw discriminatory employment practices by private firms receiving contracts from state governments.
3. Laws to provide equal opportunity for all state employees, modeled after the federal government's affirmative action executive order.

4. Laws forbidding discrimination because of age, patterned after the Federal Age Discrimination Act.

Broad as their coverage may appear to be, lack of adequate funds and enforcement personnel have, as in the case of state commissions against discrimination, hindered the effective implementation of these laws.

Each of the New England states has a Governor's Commission on the Status of Women, which provides information on laws affecting equal opportunity for women. Their resources are very limited. The highest budget in New England, $30,000 in 1975, is that of the Massachusetts commission. A proposal for matching federal grants, long recommended to increase the resources of these commissions, has not been passed by Congress.

The Impact of National Policy

Increasing awareness of the inadequacy of the state laws[7] led to a growing movement in support of federal legislation, which culminated in the 1960s in the creation of the national Equal Employment Opportunity Commission and to federal contract compliance and equal employment opportunity orders.

A battery of federal legislation[8] has been enacted in recent years to provide women with equal opportunities and pay. The Equal Pay Act (1963) forbids paying women less than men for comparable work. Title VII of the Civil Rights Act of 1964, administered by the Equal Employment Opportunity Commission, guarantees equal employment opportunities for women and minorities by prohibiting unfair employment practices (in hiring, firing, promotions, and fringe benefits). Executive Orders 11246 and 11375 and Revised Order 4 require companies and institutions with federal contracts and the federal government itself to eliminate discrimination and provide affirmative action programs to guarantee equal employment opportunities. Equal educational opportunities are now guaranteed by Title IX of the Education Amendments Act of 1972.[9]

Despite all the legislation, analyses of aggregate data show no discernible improvement in the pay or employment status of women or minorities in recent years, although small changes have been introduced by some industries and firms. The analysis below, which includes the criticisms made by the United States Civil Rights Commission,[10] suggests some of the reasons for this apparent failure to implement public policy.

Equal Pay Act

Legislation requiring equal pay for equal or comparable work regardless of the sex of the employee was passed by some states as early as 1919. Organized labor allied with national women's groups pushed for federal legislation during the 1930s and 1940s. In 1963, President John F. Kennedy signed the Equal Pay Act, an amendment to the 1938 Fair Labor Standards Act (which provides minimum wages and maximum hours for certain classifications of employees). Amendments have broadened the coverage of the Fair Labor Standards Act so that today it covers more than seventy million women and men.

Despite a few rulings requiring back pay to compensate for past discrimination, the legislation has had little overall impact on wage differentials, both because of the law itself and the way it has been administered. The law does not address the issue of women and men working in entirely separate categories of work in which their productive efforts may be similar but their pay unequal. Yet this type of what has come to be termed occupational segregation is responsible for a major portion of the wage differences between men and women workers. Beyond that, the law has not been adequately enforced even as it stands.

Enforcement procedures. If a woman has reason to believe that her pay is not equal to that of a man doing comparable work, she may file a complaint by phoning the appropriate labor department regional office or branch. The department's review may include all pay practices in the firm or plant. The complainant's privacy is respected unless the complaint reaches court, which occurs in only 5 percent of the cases. Since the enactment of the law, New England firms found in violation of the act have had to pay $85 million to aggrieved women workers.

Despite these rulings, the laws have led to little change in overall industry hiring and upgrading practices affecting women workers. Large firms have "desexed" their pay grade levels, eliminating female and male job distinctions. But they continue to hire women in the five or six lowest levels, while assigning men to the higher ones. The issue of whether, in fact, the work done by women in the categories to which they are assigned is equal in value to that done by men has not been tackled.

The regional administrator of the Equal Pay Act in New England reports difficulty in persuading women to file complaints. While there was a sharp increase in complaints in second quarter of 1975, for example, the actual number was only 200, 0.01 percent of the two million women covered by the act in the region. Critics of the act point out that to rely on the victims of discrimination to make complaints is unlikely to be effective because their low pay and job insecurity render delay and fear of reprisal major deterrents to action on their part.

Problems in administration. The Equal Pay Act has given the Department of Labor three broad powers: to investigate, to conciliate where violations are found, and to litigate where efforts to secure compliance have failed. As of September 1975, there were a total of 979 compliance officers in the Wage and Hour Division of the Employment Standards Administration in New England. They spent only 10 percent of their time on Equal Pay Act (EPA) complaints and the remainder on minimum wage, overtime, child labor, and related violations.

The Commission on Civil Rights points out that the national Equal Pay Act staff has not been adequately expanded to cope with its growing task. Although the number of complaints multiplied seven times from 1959 to 1974, its national staff remained about the same size.[11] Despite the 1972 reorganization, the Civil Rights Commission adds, there is no formal mechanism for coordinating EPA enforcement nationally. This is left to assistant regional directors. The

New England solicitor's office, responsible for prosecuting court action, allocates about 25 percent of its time to the Equal Pay Act, giving one attorney the primary responsibility for handling all cases under it.

There are inconsistencies between Equal Pay Act policies and those of the Equal Employment Opportunity Commission. Equal Pay Act administrators, in contrast to those in the EEOC, have ruled that pension plans for men and women do not have to be equal in every respect; maternity benefits are not wages and do not come under sex discrimination guidelines; and employee training in some cases may be made available to men and not to women. Part-time workers, the majority of whom are female, may be paid lower hourly wages than full-time workers.

The Civil Rights Commission concludes:

> Failure to publish uniform, clear, and specific instructions may have effectively prevented employers from complying with the law. In addition, female professionals may have been denied the hope of reaching out-of-court settlements with employers because of the vagueness of the guidelines.[12]

Administration of the Equal Pay Act also falls short in other ways. Complaints are backlogged (1,600 by the end of fiscal year 1974). It takes three months to begin an investigation and an average of nine to complete one. Conciliation agreements are frequently reached with employers without the knowledge of the employee who is faced with a *fait accompli* and must decide whether to accept the decision. If she does not accept, she must proceed against the employer on her own and may not accept back pay awarded by the conciliation settlement.

Women's organizations have criticized the administration of the Equal Pay Act for inadequate investigations and settlements. In 1974, despite the fact that almost 700 cases were referred from regional offices for court enforcement, only 177 lawsuits were actually filed. Referral of cases to the Department of Justice for criminal prosecution, reserved for "flagrant violators," has yet to take place.

Title VII of the Civil Rights Act of 1964:
The Equal Employment Opportunity Commission (EEOC)

Title VII of the 1964 Civil Rights Act covers all those who work in establishments with fourteen or more employees, all state and local government employees, and all those who belong to labor unions with fourteen or more members. The purpose of Title VII is to end discriminatory employment practices, which include hiring, firing, promotion, wages, testing, training, and apprenticeship.

As originally conceived, the commission was to be the tool to accomplish what state commissions had failed to do. It was expected to initiate complaints and to have cease and desist power that would make it effective. Congressional opposition resulted in a compromise, however, which withheld from the commission the power to issue cease and desist orders. The commission, with powers added to it by 1972 legislation, may: (1) investigate charges of discrimination; (2) resolve complaints through conciliation; (3) file and prosecute lawsuits against respondents when conciliation fails; (4) file, through its commissioners, charges against respondents and conduct hearings; and (5) require employers of 100 or more persons to file yearly reports on the make-up of their work force. This material, however, may not be made available to the public.

To file a complaint under Title VII, the complainant obtains a form from an EEOC office and files it with that office. Where state commissions against discrimination exist, all charges over which they have jurisdiction are referred to them for a period of sixty days. If the state agency does not resolve the complaint, the EEOC investigates and seeks an agreement. If none is obtained, suit may be brought in federal district court.

EEOC began its operations with a backlog, which has increased each year so that it now totals more than 100,000 cases. The median time for resolution of complaints is 32 months. In New England, there are about 2,550 cases pending before the commission. About 35 percent of these are sex discrimination cases.

Basically, the EEOC is a conciliation rather than an enforcement agency for individual complaints. The broad consent decrees that have been reached through EEOC have covered large numbers of people and provided considerable sums in back pay, but the Civil Rights Commission has criticized two of the most important.

> The AT&T agreement . . . suffers from insufficient monitoring and follow-up, and the steel industry decree has been criticized because the affected classes of employees are excluded from the negotiations and it calls for the government to make an appearance on behalf of the industry, should an employee bring a private suit. [13]

In the summer of 1977, the Supreme Court handed down several rulings that further restricted the interpretation of Title VII of the Civil Rights Act. The court held that absence caused by pregnancy could not be compensated for as a disability, and "bona fide" seniority systems need not be altered although they perpetuate employment patterns discriminating against women or minorities. [14] The implications of these interpretations have not yet been fully worked out.

Federal Contract Compliance

Criticisms of fair employment programs in the 1960s emphasized the need to end patterns of discrimination rather than simply respond to individual complaints. An executive order has since established federal contract compliance that requires all those who obtain government contracts to be equal opportunity employers. Written affirmative action programs must be prepared and implemented by educational institutions and companies that have yearly federal contracts exceeding $50,000. About 40 percent of the working population is employed by such contractors, including all employees of a large number of educational institutions, almost all banks and insurance companies, and many private companies that sell goods and services to the federal government. The federal order is administered by the Office of Federal Contract Compliance Programs (OFCCP).

Office of Federal Contract Compliance Programs (OFCCP). The OFCCP, located in the Department of Labor, has overall supervision of the administration of contract compliance programs, which are carried out by twelve agencies and departments: Treasury; Health, Education, and Welfare; Housing and Urban Development; Interior; Transportation; Defense; Veterans Administration; Agriculture; Commerce; Environmental Protection Agency; the Energy Research and Development Administration; and the General Services Administration.

Complaints about contract compliance are filed with the appropriate contracting agency. The Department of Health, Education, and Welfare, for example, handles all complaints relating to educational institutions. Complaints may also be made directly to the labor department's Office of Contract Compliance Programs, which is located in each region's Employment Standards Administration office.

Criticism of the OFCCP. Women's organizations, the Commission on Civil Rights, and federal policy makers have all criticized the administration of contract compliance. The opinion of the Boston regional OFCCP administrator, shared by many, is that affirmative action as a tool to expand career options for women and minorities is "at a sixth grade level." Methods of insuring that companies formulate and implement affirmative action programs, provided for by its regulations, have not been fully utilized. Pre-award review for possible discriminatory practices are mandatory for contracts over $1 million, but these have been either cursory or not made at all. Only nine companies were debarred from receiving contracts because of discrimination in the ten years until 1975. The withholding of progress payments was authorized in April 1973, but, as of February 1975, no contractor had been denied funds for failure to adopt or abide by an affirmative action program despite the filing of many complaints and findings of employment discrimination.

Each regional office of the OFCCP is supposed to have copies of contracting companies' affirmative action programs. Companies may, however, claim they are confidential so that only parts of them may be inspected by the public.

The Office of Federal Contract Compliance is three steps removed from the secretary of labor, too distant to have any impact on major department policy. The office deputy assistant secretary is responsible to the assistant secretary for employment standards who is, in turn, responsible to the undersecretary of labor.

The budget allocations for handling enforcement per contractor varies significantly as between the differing federal departments and agencies, suggesting a lack of uniformity in enforcement procedures. The allocation per contractor in 1971 ranged from $1,688 (NASA) to $46 (Department of Agriculture). Expenditures per contractor-employee range from $2 in the Department of Commerce to less than nine cents in the Department of Health, Education, and Welfare.

HEW's Office for Civil Rights (OCR)

Supervision of the antidiscrimination executive order as it relates to educational institutions with government contracts has been delegated to the Office for Civil Rights of the Department of Health, Education, and Welfare. Partly as a result of a long delay in the development and dissemination of regulations, and partly because of inefficient handling of complaints in regional offices, the overall record of OCR in promoting affirmative action is very poor.

Little attempt has been made to improve the employment status of women in colleges and universities. Shortly before the end of fiscal 1975, OCR threatened to withhold government contracts from 29 universities and colleges if they did not sign "model" affirmative action plans based on the so-called Berkeley Plan under which the University of California at Berkeley agreed to add 100 women and minority group members to its 1,500 person faculty over a thirty-year period. Women's and minority organizations had severely criticized the inadequacies of the model. In any case the Office of Civil Rights withdrew the threat so that even this token gesture came to naught.

In fact, no educational institutions have had federal funds withheld. Thousands of complaints of sex discrimination filed against colleges and universities have been neither heard nor settled. The relatively few women who have received satisfactory resolution of complaints have had to resort to court proceedings.

OCR is also responsible for enforcing Title IX of the Education Amendments of 1972. Title IX covers all educational institutions that receive federal money and, with a few exceptions, requires equity in admissions, in treatment of students, in vocational education, and in undergraduate and graduate programs.

Since Title IX regulations were not finally adopted until the summer of 1975, compliance is still at a beginning stage. Like all other laws, much depends on the way it is administered and enforced. A citizens' group known as PEER[15] (Project on Equal Educational Rights) suggests that to conform with Title IX, school districts should (1) appoint and publicize the name of its Title IX coordinator, (2) notify all students and employees that it does not discriminate on the basis of sex, (3) start reviewing its programs and policies for sex discrimination, and (4) develop a grievance procedure for resolving sex discrimination problems.[16] Colleges and universities must appoint representatives to insure that they are in conformance with Title IX regarding admissions and equal treatment for students.

Affirmative Action for Federal Employees

An executive order requires affirmative action programs for minorities and women within each federal department and agency. Equal employment opportunity officers, called federal women's coordinators, are located in each regional office to enforce these programs.

The federal government has, however, so far failed to become a "model employer." Statistics show only very small increases in the number of women employed at the middle or top management level since the program's start in the late 1960s.

The Civil Service Commission, responsible for administering affirmative action in the federal government, has failed to promote the program effectively. It permits federal agencies to investigate and judge their own performance. Since agencies have been reluctant to undertake or profit from self-criticism, a widespread lack of confidence in the complaint procedures has developed. The Civil Rights Commission maintains that the Civil Service Commission's own personnel procedures, including recruitment, selection, and promotion, discriminate against minorities and women.

Congressional criticism, following hearings in 1971, led to legislation designed to put more teeth into equal opportunity employment in the federal civil service. The Civil Service Commission was to review and approve the affirmative action plans of all government departments and agencies annually. Federal employees were given the right to sue in federal district court for settlement of individual grievances.

The Commission on Civil Rights found, however, that there had been no systematic review of employment practices. The Civil Service Commission had not "moved to bring any of its own standards into conformity with the standards required of private and state and local government employers under Title VII." The Civil Service Commission guidelines for federal departments and agencies are actually weaker than those required for private employers under contract compliance regulations. Agencies have not bothered to submit their affirmative action plans on time, and proper reporting devices have not been developed.

Civil Rights Commission Recommendation

The Civil Rights Commission's 1974 report concludes that the federal effort is inadequate due to "lack of overall leadership and direction, the diffusion of responsibility to a number of agencies, the existence of inconsistent policies and standards, the absence of joint investigative or enforcement strategies, and the failure of the agencies covered in this report to develop strong compliance programs."[17]

The commission therefore urged the establishment of a single comprehensive agency, perhaps to be called the National Employment Rights Board, with a unified standard of compliance. The board would have administrative and litigative authority and the right to act on its own initiative without having to wait until complaints are received.[18] The commission proposed the new agency's budget should be one and one-half times the amount currently spent on the federal government's total enforcement efforts. Whether and how such an agency should be established has not yet been decided. A government task force has been created to consider the whole issue.

Additional Resources

The regional director of the Women's Bureau of the Department of Labor is a major potential source of assistance to women seeking to expand career options. The Women's Bureau, with limited funds, is responsible for formulating standards and policies which shall promote the welfare of wage earning women, improve their working conditions, increase their efficiency, advance their opportunities for professional employment, and investigate and report on all matters pertinent to the welfare of women in industry. It offers material on employment options for women and is primarily an informative, rather than a service, agency. It has sponsored several meetings, both nationally and regionally, on women and employment.

The federal government funds a wide range of projects relating to jobs for women. Most of these grants and contracts have been allocated through the Health, Education, and Welfare department's Office of Education.[19] Every year, the HEW issues guidelines under which interested groups may apply for these funds. Unfortunately, the public has not been involved in or made privy to the kind of critical evaluation needed to determine the overall impact of these grants and contracts.

Part 2
Barriers Confronting Wage Earning Women in New England

4

The Women Who Work for Pay

Why Women Work

A high proportion of women who work for pay do so because they must help support their families. Some are the sole support of their families. This point was underscored by the participants in Workshop I on women seeking to enter the paid labor force for the first time or to re-enter it after their children are in school (see Fig. 4.1).

The increased participation of women in the paid labor force reflects, in part, the impact of technology in removing many kinds of work from the home to the market over the last half century. Inside the home, the time required to perform household tasks has been potentially reduced by technological innovation: electric refrigerators and packaged and frozen foods, washing and drying machines, ready-to-wear synthetic fabrics, and vacuum cleaners. But all these innovations cost money. Families need higher incomes to buy them.

Outside the home, technological advance has increased the demand for unskilled and semi-skilled labor, creating greater opportunities for paying jobs for women from low income families.

In 1974, 43 percent of all women in the United States who were married and living with their husbands were working in paying jobs. In other words, in nearly half the families in the country, both the husband and the wife were working to earn money.[1] The wage earning wife typically contributes 20 to 40 percent of the familiy income.[2] Some mothers stop working when they have children. Many do not.

50

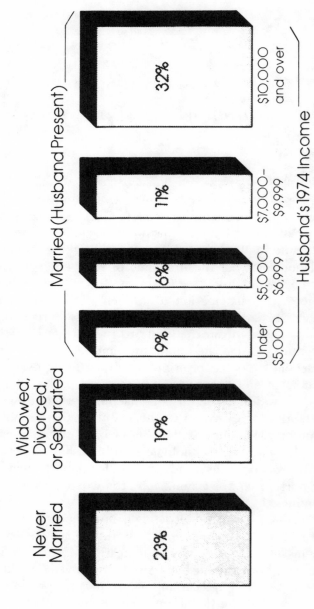

Figure 4.1 Women in the labor force, by marital status, March 1973. Most women work because of economic need. Source: U.S., Department of Labor, Employment Standards Administration, Women's Bureau; data from U.S., Department of Labor, Bureau of Labor Statistics.

In New England, half of all women between the ages of 18 and 64 were working for pay by 1970. Only during the childbearing years, 25 to 34, did this proportion drop to about four out of ten. One mother out of four with children under six continues to work for pay in Massachusetts and Connecticut. A higher proportion, one out of three, remains in the paid labor force in the less industrialized states of New Hampshire, Vermont, and Maine, where men's wages tend to be lower. More women in New England, two out of five, go back to wage employment when their children, between 6 and 18 years old, are in school. The proportion is higher in the rural northern tier states.

A far higher proportion of women who head their families must work for pay as the primary source of family income. Over the past two and one-half decades, one-parent families headed by women have been growing more rapidly than husband-wife families.[3] The large increase in female-headed families reflects the increase in the number of separated and divorced women. The increasing economic independence of women may contribute in part to marital instability.[4] Recent high levels of unemployment have also aggravated family conflicts and further increased the divorce rate. Nationally, three-fourths of all divorcees and over half of all women married but whose husbands were absent were in the labor force in 1974.[5]

In March 1975, one in eight families nationally (7.2 million families) was headed by a woman.[6] The incomes of these families were about half those of families where both husband and wife were present. Nearly half of the women family heads, aged 25 to 44, have three or more children.[7] A high percentage of women family heads hold paid jobs in New England (see Table 4.1).

Societal institutions make little or no allowance for the special problems these women confront as mothers and as the main providers of financial support for their children. Divorced, separated women and widows, desperately in need of paid employment to support their families, often find the failure to prepare adequately for careers when they were younger has left them ill-equipped for jobs other than those

Table 4.1

Percentage of Women Heads of Family Who Had Paying Jobs in New England in 1970

	(as % of all women family heads)	(as % of all women on paid labor force)
Connecticut	61	7
Maine	55	5
Massachusetts	57	7
New Hampshire	62	8
Rhode Island	55	6
Vermont	59	9

Source: Calculated from U. S., Department of Commerce, Census of the Population, 1970 (Washington, D.C., Government Printing Office, 1970), "Characteristics of Population (by State)", Table 22.

requiring little education and skill. Many ultimately end up on welfare rolls. The 1975 *Manpower Report of the President* points out that, for many, the high cost of child care and low earnings reduce the feasibility of paid employment and, in many cases, make it uneconomical.[8]

Welfare mothers constitute a group with few rights and little ability to push for better status in the paid labor market. They often face a dilemma. Their welfare payments are insufficient to maintain their families, but they lose part of their meager income if they seek to supplement it by taking a paid job. It is, of course, impossible to know how many of these women work illicitly at menial, low-paying jobs merely to survive, but estimates suggest that nationally the numbers run into the hundreds of thousands.

In the last twenty years, on the other hand, employment opportunities have increased for better educated women. They have become increasingly likely to enter paid employment. This may reflect their desire to buy more of the modern appliances that make housework easier, their wish to provide their families with a wider range of leisure activities including sports and cultural events, or their concern that their children have better and more education, especially at the post-high school level. It may also reflect their desire to enter what they hope will be a more stimulating world of work, especially after their children have started school. The typical pattern today for a woman with a bachelor's degree or above is to obtain a job, leave it while her children are young for a period of years, and then return to the paid labor force for a prolonged period, as many as thirty years, before she retires.

The Socialization Process

The participants in every workshop referred to the deep-rooted socialization process that shapes every aspect of a woman's life perspectives, influencing not only the decision-making processes that determine the kinds of paid jobs available to her, but also her own ability and willingness to improve her career options. At home, little girls are constantly reminded to behave like mommy; little boys, like daddy. In lower grades at school, girls are usually encouraged to think of themselves as housewives and mothers or, at most, school teachers and nurses. They are seldom encouraged to plan and develop careers that involve extensive training and long-term commitment to advancement in the paid labor force, despite the fact that today one out of two will probably spend a major portion of her life working for pay. Few if any courses help women understand why it is important to participate in and acquire the skills for collective bargaining.

Once a woman reaches an institution of higher learning, she finds the facilities needed to enable her to continue her education are sorely lacking. Her needs may vary, depending on her family status, whether she is entering right after college, has young children, or is returning to study after her children have entered school. Typically, the kinds of programs required to assist her, whatever her own particular circumstances are, are not available: fewer funds are available for women students; child care is seldom available; flexible programs that might enable her to raise a family while she is studying are often frowned upon; and released time from current jobs to obtain advanced training is difficult for her to obtain.[9]

The informal education provided by the communications media plays a major role in socializing men and women to

accept the myth that women's place is still in the home.
Women are seldom portrayed in roles where they exercise
leadership, either in paid work or in the community. Instead,
they are typically portrayed as housewives and/or sex ob-
jects.[10] The ad in which the fatuous man proclaims, "My
wife, I think I'll keep her," summed up the ignominious
status of women presented by most of the media, even today.

The surrounding institutions and practices of the community at large further perpetuate the myth that women's
place is still in the home. Tax and social security legislation,
even the methods of paying unemployment compensation,
discriminate against women who work for pay. The list is too
long to include here, but the point was repeatedly stressed at
the workshops that institutionalized societal practices function at almost every level to sanction, and in this sense to
"teach," the myth that women should plan to devote themselves to home and family.

The Double Burden of Household Work

Although more and more women have taken paid jobs because of economic necessity, many are constrained in the
kinds of jobs they may take because their fathers, husbands,
brothers, and children expect them, even while they are
earning money, to perform most household duties as well.[11]
In some cases, adolescents, especially teen-age girls, may take
over the housekeeping responsibilities while their mothers go
out to work.[12]

The burden of household duties frequently limits women,
especially those in the lower income brackets, to paid jobs
that place little demand on their time outside normal working hours. This tends to discourage many from entering certain occupations and professions where hours are long,
demands are heavy, and training periods are extended.

An important substitute for the housewife, available only
to higher income families, is domestic labor. Although the number of women in domestic service has declined relatively over
the years, the persistence of a pool of unskilled women seeking
paid jobs has helped make it easier for more well-to-do wom-
en to take advantage of job opportunities outside the home.

The Role of Myths in the Job Market

In the world of paid work, the myth that women are only working temporarily enables employers and male employees to rationalize practices and attitudes that operate daily to push them into the least skilled, lowest paying jobs. The myth influences employers' decisions shaping job opportunities for women and men in three sometimes contradictory respects.

First, they tend automatically to perceive men as the best candidates for key decision-making posts at the supervisory and managerial level,[13] since men are still considered more likely than women to remain in the paid labor force. This is reinforced by the fact that boys are counseled to plan their careers and are given more opportunities to obtain the necessary education to enter higher level jobs before they enter the work force. On the job, supervisors are more likely to encourage men and to enable them to acquire on-the-job training.

From 1960 to 1970, there was actually a relative decline in the proportion of women employed at the management and administrative level, especially in the private sector, despite the overall increase of female employment.[14]

Secondly, the myth provides employers with a ready rationalization for failure to provide women with clearly defined upgrading, on-the-job training, or higher wages in periods of expanding demand for labor. When demand slackens and output falls, employers rationalize laying women off before men for similar reasons. In some instances, women have been hired to replace men in traditional men's jobs when the men have demanded wages considered too high. This practice tends to come to public notice primarily where women have been hired to replace men during strikes. Historically, it was a significant factor bolstering trade union efforts to exclude women from employment in particular fields altogether.[15]

The myths about women workers have undoubtedly played a role in forming the new patterns of employment that have emerged with the technological advances and structural shifts in the economy in recent years. Employers commonly do not attempt to estimate labor costs when new

technologies are introduced, for typically they do not increase. On the one hand, economies of scale accompanying
innovation have contributed to growing concentration and
domination of the United States economy by multinational
corporations. These have tended increasingly to shift
assembly and last stage processing to less developed countries
where legislation restricting effective unionization, together
with chronic unemployment and rural poverty, generate a far
larger and lower-cost labor reserve than that available in the
United States.[16] Thus traditionally low-paying women's
industries like textiles and electronics have lost hundreds of
thousands of jobs to areas like Singapore, Taiwan, Korea,
Mexico, Brazil, and South Africa. Wages in South African
factories, for example, where four out of five United States
dollars invested in African manufacturing industries are
located, are about one-sixth of the wages paid to women in
comparable work in the United States, and profits are almost
double.[17]

On the other hand, the introduction of new technologies
in the growing distribution and service sectors have permitted
employment of more routinized lower cost labor requiring
less skills. These have been the jobs into which the rapidly
growing numbers of women workers have been encouraged to
move in recent years, not only in New England, but also
throughout the United States.

At the level of employee reaction to employment decisions, the myth that women may be expected to remain at
home has encouraged male workers, who fear potential female competition for jobs they consider "theirs," to try to
exclude women from union membership and/or from
apprenticeship training programs.[18] This, historically, has
been especially true of crafts unions, whose primary strength
has traditionally rested in their ability to restrict entry.

Only a little over 10 percent of women wage workers
have been organized in unions nationally, compared to over
30 percent of male workers. For the most part, female union
membership is concentrated in factory employment. Women
in the more rapidly expanding clerical, sales, and service
worker categories outside the public sector, tend to be almost

Table 4.2

Median Weekly Earnings of Full-Time Wage and Salary Workers by Selected Characteristics and Union or Non-Union Status, May 1974

| | Median Weekly Earnings | | | Union/ Non-Union | |
	All Workers	Union Members	Non-Union Workers	Percentage Differential	Percentage in Unions
Full-time workers	$169	$202	$157	28.7	26.8
Men	204	215	194	10.8	32.2
Women	124	145	120	20.8	16.5
White workers	173	206	162	27.2	26.2
Men	209	219	201	9.0	31.5
Women	125	146	122	19.7	15.8
Black workers	140	169	124	36.3	31.4
Men	160	183	141	29.8	38.4
Women	117	141	110	28.2	21.2

Source: T. F. Bradshaw and J.F. Stimson, "Trends in Weekly Earnings: An Analysis", in Monthly Labor Review, August 1975.

entirely unorganized.

The fact that so few women have joined unions may be, in part, the result of another type of socialization that has led many to ignore available evidence indicating that women in unions have earned significantly higher wages than those not in unions (see Table 4.2). Like men, women wage earners read press stories almost daily that single out corruption in unions but seldom report facts showing that unions have improved wage and working conditions. Women's attitudes may be further influenced by their own particular socialization to the effect that participation in unions is not "lady-like." This belief is fostered by the attitude often adopted by white collar workers in general (including clerical and sales workers, the fastest growing employment categories for women) that to join unions is beneath them. Employers often encourage this attitude, arguing that white collar workers, despite their relatively low wages, are really part of management.

There is, however, considerable evidence that unions

themselves, for the most part dominated by men, have not made adequate efforts to develop appropriate techniques for organizing the fast-growing numbers of women workers, especially in the newer areas where their employment is expanding rapidly. The failure of unions to devote special attention to organizing women may, as some workshop participants suggested, be more of a general failure of the leadership to mobilize all workers.[19] Consideration of this possibility is outside the scope of this book, but it may be that as long as unions fail to deal effectively with ideologies which, like sexism, tend to divide workers, it is unlikely they will be able to increase their membership and play a more effective role as a countervailing power in collective bargaining for better wages and conditions for either men or women.

The Triple Jeopardy of Black and Other Minority Women

Black and other minority[1] women must enter paid employment in higher proportions than other women primarily because of economic need. Nevertheless, they are typically shunted into the lowest paid, least attractive jobs. Most participants of the second workshop agreed that these women are thrice jeopardized[2] by racism, classism,[3] and sexism.

Who Are the Minority Women in New England?

Although there were relatively few minority women in New England, a number of factors have combined in recent decades to increase their numbers sharply. Figure 5.1 shows the percentage of women who were classified by the census as belonging to the "other race" or "minority" category in the six New England states in 1970.[4]

Blacks constitute the largest single minority group in New England today. Although they constitute a smaller percentage of the regional population than in many other regions of the nation, they make up a considerably higher proportion (almost one-fifth) of the inner-city populations of the three more industrialized states: Massachusetts, Connecticut, and Rhode Island. About half live in Connecticut, particularly in the bigger cities like Hartford, New Haven, and Stamford. Most of the rest live in Massachusetts (44 percent). The largest single group of blacks in New England is concentrated in Boston.

The minority population of New England has grown rapidly in the past quarter of a century. The labor shortages

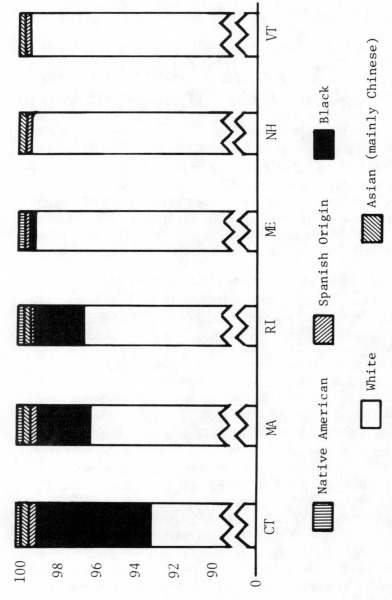

Figure 5.1 Percentage of women who are minorities in New England, 1970. Source: U.S., Department of Commerce, *Census of Population, 1970* (Washington, D.C., Government Printing Office, 1970), "Characteristics of Population (by State)," Table 19.

during World War II created new employment opportunities for blacks, particularly males, who migrated from the South. After the war, mechanization pushed many entire families out of southern agriculture.

The black women who migrated to New England with their families after World War II discovered that, even there, discriminatory practices thwarted their efforts to obtain better jobs and earn higher pay. From the outset, their choices even as to where they could live were narrowly determined; discriminatory housing, as well as restricted incomes, forced the vast majority to crowd into the inner cities of the largest metropolitan areas.[5]

The rapid growth of Boston's black population illustrates the pattern and impact of this process which, over the past quarter of a century, transformed a large portion of the nation's blacks from a southern, rural people into a northern, urban, industrial working class. From 1950 to 1960, blacks, as a proportion of Boston's population, doubled from 5 to almost 10 percent; over 80 percent of them concentrated in Boston itself. The more affluent white population had begun to move out to the suburbs. The executive director of the Urban League declared: "it hardly appears debatable that the trend toward the building of racial ghettos in . . . Massachusetts is clearly established and well underway."[6]

By 1970, the trend toward ghettoization had become even more pronounced. The proportion of blacks in Boston had risen to over 16 percent of the city's 640,000 inhabitants, far more than all the other identified minorities combined. Within the city, most peoples of color had become restricted to a few areas like Roxbury and Dorchester. The proportion of blacks has, since 1970, grown to more than 20 percent.

Economic necessity has forced a higher proportion of black women than other women to enter the paid labor force. A primary factor is that black men tend to receive lower wages and suffer higher rates of unemployment than most other men because of the pervasive discriminatory practices and discouragement they confront.[7]

Second, a higher proportion of black families are headed

by women than is the case for other groups, so that many black women must obtain jobs as the primary support of their families. The percentage of female-headed black families is increasing nationally and has almost doubled in slightly more than two decades from 17.6 percent in 1950 to 28.9 percent in 1970.[8] This contrasts to 8.5 and 9.4 percent among white families in the same years.

In 1973, women headed 73 percent of all black families with incomes below poverty level in Boston. This was the highest proportion of female-headed families in any group in any city in the nation.[9] More research is needed to explain why this should be the case.

There is considerable debate as to the causes and implications of the fact that a high proportion of black families is headed by women.[10] Whatever the cause, most scholars agree that this partly explains the high proportion of black women seeking paid jobs. It should be emphasized, however, that the higher the incomes of a black family, the less likely it is that it will be headed by a woman. At an income of $15,000 or more, the proportion of black, female-headed families is about the same as that of whites. At lower incomes, on the other hand, the number of black families headed by women rises quickly. The additional economic pressures imposed by low family incomes apparently contribute to throwing a greater responsibility on black women.

Spanish-speaking Americans are, next to blacks, the second largest minority in New England. This category is, unfortunately, not broken down further in the census, and it is not entirely clear which groups are included. There is a long-resident community of Cape Verdeans: persons of mixed African and Portuguese descent from the Cape Verde Islands who became established in eastern Massachusetts and Rhode Island in the nineteenth century. Some came as sailors, including prosperous ship captains, who purchased land and homes. A number maintained the cultural traditions and even the African and Portuguese languages of their ancestors.

A number of Spanish-speaking people have migrated to New England more recently, especially since World War II.[11] For the most part, they, too, live in the biggest cities.

Boston's Hispanic population multiplied from 644 in 1960 to 17,984 in 1970. A recent survey showed that 150,030 Spanish people now live in Massachusetts, about one-third of them in Boston. Close to half of these are Puerto Ricans who, as citizens, have no difficulty entering the United States. Others come from other Latin American countries, from which entry is more difficult.

Like many of their European predecessors, they came to escape their impoverished homelands. Many arrived by plane, their fares paid by local companies seeking low-cost labor. They are unskilled workers entering a highly industrialized, specialized economy, in which there is a premium on acquired technical skills. They know little English. Their customs are different. Their experience with an integrated society ill-prepares them for the racially and economically stratified communities of the big New England cities where they, like blacks, must live in ghettos. Noncitizens, who cannot obtain welfare, must sometimes hold two and three jobs to earn enough to subsist.

Many circumstances may hinder a Puerto Rican woman from seeking paid work, no matter how desperately her family may need her meager wage. Often she has small children who need her care and attention. Three-fourths of all Puerto Rican families in the United States have children under eighteen years of age. Almost one-third of all Puerto Ricans living on the mainland are under ten years old. Spanish is the language spoken in about three-fourths of their homes. Since child care facilities are not geared to the language and cultural needs of her children, the Puerto Rican mother must often either stay home to care for them or send them back to relatives in Puerto Rico. A woman heads one out of three mainland Puerto Rican families, far more than among the general population. For her, a paid job is vital. Yet she lacks sufficient education and training to earn a decent salary. She is often unable to read and write English, even if she can speak it. A more basic problem is that of maintaining her own identity in the context of the dominant community. As Miranda Lourdes King declares,

always present are the subtle pressures of finding her values
as a Puerto Rican threatened and misunderstood. Since her
livelihood depends on it, she has to prove herself constantly—
among men and women—in the larger society, straining to
conform.[12]

Cubans, the second largest group of Hispanic people
in New England today, tend to be better off. Because of
its anti-Castro stance, Congress passed laws to provide many
Cubans with airlifts and special welfare programs. Agencies
were established to help them make the transition. Many are
professionals who rapidly moved from factory to white collar
jobs, once they learned English.

Asians, mainly Chinese, constitute another important
minority in the industrialized New England states. They,
too, confront prejudices that have a long history. Many
stereotypes emerged in the anti-Chinese period of 1870–
1900, when Chinese men were imported to provide low-
cost contract labor to build the transcontinental railroads.
For a long time, Chinese women were excluded from the
United States. In New England, the numbers of Chinese
women have only in very recent years come to equal those of
men.

There is little information about the job status or incomes of Asians in New England. Only now are researchers
beginning to examine these issues. Available data indicate
that Asians, too, are concentrated in urban centers. In
Boston, for example, most Chinese live in the congested area
called Chinatown where they maintain a fairly closely knit
community. Some of the more recent immigrants, a high
proportion of them women, still do not speak or read
English.

Other Asian groups are fewer in number and do not
live in as easily identifiable groups. Little has been written on
the problems confronting these women in paid employment.
Nevertheless, it is clear that the attitudes and practices of the
dominant culture also restrict their career choices.

Native Americans are reported by the census to constitute barely a tenth of one percent of the population of any

New England state except Maine, where they make up two-tenths. Death in wars to defend their land, and westward and northern migration to escape the foreign intruders, as well as decimation by unfamiliar diseases introduced by the colonists, drastically reduced their initial population base. Beyond that, early intermixing and adoption of the ways of colonial settlers, including intermarriage, caused many to "disappear" from census enumerations.[13]

The census data misrepresent the size of the Native American population in New England. Though it appears to have multiplied four to five times since 1950, this is really a consequence of census-taking methodology. Until 1960, the census takers, instead of asking for ethnic identification, made their own determination as to "race." The historical intermingling of various communities in New England made such determinations extremely difficult, so there was extensive under-reporting of Native Americans in the earlier censuses. For example, many Narragansetts, who had numbered thousands and occupied most of Rhode Island in the sixteenth century, were enslaved along with blacks on colonial plantations in Rhode Island, Massachusetts, and Connecticut. By the nineteenth century, Narragansetts had become difficult to distinguish from other groups.

> So much mixture has taken place . . . that persons of Narragansett descent range in appearance from White to Negro. Most individuals fall between the few extremes, with a few who "look like Indians."[14]

Only in Maine were a significant number still identified as "Indian" in the census.

Despite their historical antecedents as owners of all the land in the region, available census data today show that most known Native Americans live, as do most other minorities, in the larger cities of New England.

Little is written about Native American women. The dominant mythology about their earlier societies, whether in legend or on television, primarily depicts male natives, conjuring up an impression of an invisible, personalityless squaw.

There is evidence that, in precolonial societies and in Native American communities today, women play an important role in community decision making. Yet they confront problems similar to those of other minorities in seeking paid jobs. Much more research is required to analyze the nature and causes of the particular sets of obstacles they face. Could they broaden their participation in the professions, however, the culture of the entire region would be much enriched.

Institutionalized Racism Combined with Sexism

The participants of the second workshop analyzed the intertwining of the institutionalized myths that disadvantage all women in paid work and racist attitudes about minority women, both of which became imbedded in the institutions that pattern their life and work in New England. The dominant "white" culture pervades all aspects of life of minority women, affecting not only the availability of employment, but also housing, education, medical care, food, small business loans, public services, and even police protection. The dominant values are internalized through formal education in the classrooms as well as the mass media.[15]

Robert Terry argues that, in the highly technological society of the United States, the concentration of powerful machines, materials, and decision making has centered power in the hands of a "club" of white males who dominate the corporate centers of power.[16] The club legitimizes itself by appealing to definitions and values assumed to be commonly shared, thus typically excluding minorities. Unfamiliar behavior is usually interpreted negatively. To avoid criticism, Terry suggests, the club misplaces the problem by placing the blame on the victim:

> Much of the social science literature and the media depict minorities as culturally deprived and unqualified. They are labeled as disadvantaged, unreliable, too aggressive, militant, or expecting too much. . . . The focus on the victim removes pressure from the club.[17]

The career choices of many black and minority women in

New England are limited by the ghetto conditions in which poverty and discrimination force most to live. The ghettos are typically in the older, run-down, overcrowded areas of the cities. In 1960, the Massachusetts Advisory Committee reported that in nine out of twelve nonwhite neighborhoods in Boston, over half the housing units were substandard. Yet the families living there had to pay about 10 percent more rent than white families for comparable homes.[18] Traffic congestion is dangerous for young children. Recreational facilities are limited and neglected.

The inadequate educational facilities characteristic of the ghettos tend to narrow the possible career choices of black and other minority women by limiting their acquisition of needed skills. The heavy reliance on the local property tax to finance education in New England tends to limit the availability of school funds in low income areas so that many schools in the inner cities are unable to provide adequate facilities to meet minority student needs.[19] Large classes and overburdened teachers mean that special problems of minority children are likely to be ignored. There is little money to hire special teachers to help children learn English as a second language. Libraries may be limited in numbers and qualities of books. Laboratories and equipment needed to enable minority girls and boys to acquire basic skills to enter science or engineering professions tend to be lacking.

Teachers, whose attitudes too often reflect the racism of the dominant culture, may overlook the special needs of minorities. They frequently advise minority children, boys as well as girls, to narrow their job horizons. They seldom encourage them to go to college.

Some of the larger cities, like Boston, have established special vocational counseling and bilingual teaching programs to help minority children overcome these problems. These programs have been somewhat enhanced in the context of efforts to integrate the inner-city schools. But much still remains to be done.[20]

Life in the ghetto offers few of the supports a woman needs to improve her career. If a young mother finds a job, her wages are often so low she cannot afford to pay for adequate child care. Convenient, inexpensive, quality child care facilities are seldom available. These problems are aggravated if the family is not facile in English, for few child care centers are geared to non-English-speaking children.

Lack of adequate transportation seriously limits the possibility for many minority women to seek employment outside the ghetto. Many lower income families cannot afford a car. Even among those who can, the man normally has first priority, typically leaving the woman to rely on public transport. This means she is often confined to seek jobs in the immediate neighborhood, competing with others in the same plight. It is difficult for her to take a job in the newer, higher paying industrial centers opening up in the suburban areas, like those on Route 128 which encircles Boston.

Firm personnel managers often stereotype ghetto dwellers as unstable and undesirable. The minority woman who manages to find transport and child care is frequently turned down without adequate examination of her competence or credentials. If tests are given, even for mechanical jobs, they are often biased against minority women from differing cultures, whose educational opportunities may have been limited. A few small firms, in fields like textiles or electronics, take advantage of the fact that women in the ghettos find it difficult to get paid jobs by opening plants in the ghetto neighborhood and paying very low wages. The women, especially those who cannot speak English, are unlikely to know how to bargain collectively to improve their conditions. Even if their wages are below the legally required minimum or safety laws are violated, they seldom know their rights, much less how to enforce them. Some of the most recent migrants (some of whom may, in fact, be illegal entrants) are afraid to complain for fear that they will be forced to leave the country altogether.

Minority women report personal experiences that dramatically illustrate how many employers, as well as other employees, behave in ways that discourage them from seeking to improve their job status. Minority women in white collar jobs tend to confront such behavior even more than those in blue collar and service work. Minority women who phone for interviews for advertised posts may be told on arrival at the office that someone else has been given the job. Written tests sometimes contain language and cultural barriers although they are irrelevant to the tasks to be performed. Supplementary oral interviews may be used as an excuse to reject a minority woman candidate, although she performed well on the written test. On the job, minority women are often shunted to less desirable work, like packing merchandise or sorting papers in back rooms, to avoid customer contact. Other employees may make disagreeable comments, but supervisors seldom do anything to prevent it. The fact that minority women in any particular line of work may be few in number or alone makes it all the harder for them to deal with these situations.

While federal job-training legislation has encouraged the enrollment of minority women in various kinds of training programs, the numbers affected in New England have so far been very small. Affirmative action requirements in recent years have led a few employers to seek out a few exceptionally qualified minority women for top token posts, but little has been done to change the status of the vast majority.

While there are relatively few women in unions outside of blue collar work in New England, the proportions of minority women in unions are even smaller. Few of those who are members are in positions of leadership. As a result, even this avenue for improved job status has tended, in most cases, to be closed. The current organization of workers in hospital employment in the larger New England cities like Boston seems to indicate, however, that new possibilities might be opening up in this direction.

Part 3

The Obstacles Confronting Women in Major Work Categories

6
Clerical Workers

Clerical Workers Increasing

Clerical occupations[1] compose the largest single female job category in the country today. Over 11 million women are employed in clerical work throughout the nation, over half a million of them in the six New England states.

Clerical employment has multiplied threefold since World War II. This expansion reflects the fundamental shift in the nation's economic structure from manufacturing industries to distributive, financial, and service organizations. As clerical work has expanded, it has become more and more a woman's job.

More than three-fourths of all New England clerical workers are concentrated in the two most industrialized states, Massachusetts and Connecticut (see Table 6.1). Over half are in the financial and distributive centers of Massachusetts. Clerical workers make up almost one out of five workers in those two states, compared to about one out of seven in the less industrialized states. About three-fourths of all clerical workers in the region are women.

Black and Hispanic women are less likely than other women with similar educational qualifications to obtain clerical jobs. The most significant exception in New England appears to be that of clerical workers with college degrees in Massachusetts. The higher proportion of highly educated black and Spanish-language women in clerical work may mean that they were excluded from jobs in the professions; such women bring higher qualifications to clerical jobs than other women.

Table 6.1

Clerical Workers in New England States, 1970

	Connecticut	Massachusetts	Maine	New Hampshire	Rhode Island	Vermont
Total clerical workers	238,138	457,863	50,611	44,128	65,450	25,639
As a percent of all workers	18.9	19.1	13.8	15.0	17.6	15.3
Total women in clerical work	179,527	339,125	37,125	32,861	47,399	19,447
As a percent of all clerical workers	75.4	74.1	73.4	74.5	72.4	75.8
As a percent of all women workers	36.9	36.6	26.5	28.7	31.3	30.8
Total minority women in clerical work	10,335	10,635	111	165	1,129	172
As a percent of all women clerical workers	5.8	3.1	-*	-*	2.4	-*
As a percent of all minority women workers	26.1	31.4	15.8	26.6	25.6	38.6

Source: U. S., Department of Labor, Employment Standards Administration, Women's Bureau, "Women Workers in (each State)", 1970; and U. S., Department of Commerce, Census of the Population, 1970 (Washington, D.C., Government Printing Office, 1970), "General Social and Economic Characteristics (by State)", Table 54.

*Less than 1%.

Relatively Declining Wages

Nowhere does the assumption that women work only for "pin money" seem to operate more effectively than in clerical work. New England women clerical workers, like their counterparts throughout the nation, earn about 60 percent of the wages of male clerical workers and considerably less than men in all blue collar occupations. In New England, moreover, women in all types of clerical jobs earn less than the national average for women in this occupation.[2]

Traditional economic theory might predict that the rapidly expanding demand for clerical workers would lead to relatively high wages for them. Instead, the wages of women clerical workers have actually declined relative to those of other women in the paid labor force. Nationally, their median wage dropped from four-fifths to less than two-thirds of those of women in professional and technical occupations in little more than a decade from 1958 to 1970. In New England, the percentage wage increases of clerical workers in recent years have been smaller than those for other workers. In Boston, for example, between 1973 and 1974, salary increases for office clerical workers (men and women) averaged 7.6 percent compared to 8.5 percent for skilled male maintenance workers and 9.1 percent for unskilled male factory workers.[3] Table 6.2 presents data showing the median earnings of women clerical workers as a percentage of those of men.

Lack of Job Security

Conventional wisdom holds that even if clerical work does not pay high wages, it offers job security. Clerical workers, it was expected, could always get a job. Once they had one, they did not have to worry about being fired or laid off. The 1970s recession, however, seriously undercut whatever special job security clerical workers may have had. The unemployment rates of women clerical workers have been increasing more rapidly than the combined rates of women in all white collar jobs. In 1970, the unemployment rate among clerical workers was 5.1 percent compared to 4.6 percent for all female white collar workers. By 1975, the situation had

Table 6.2

Earnings in Clerical Work in New England States, 1970

	Connecticut	Massachusetts	Maine	New Hampshire	Rhode Island	Vermont
Median earnings (worked 50-52 weeks)						
Female	$5,257	$5,159	$4,300	$4,506	$4,600	$4,521
Male	8,348	7,857	7,206	7,504	7,419	7,457
Female as a percent of male	63.0%	65.7%	59.7%	60.0%	62.0%	60.6%
Median earnings (worked 50-52 weeks) Females in five largest clerical occupations						
Miscellaneous	$5,190	$5,086	$4,181	$4,405	$4,575	$4,320
Secretaries	5,636	5,557	4,486	4,858	4,938	5,111
Typists	5,190	4,901	4,314	4,291	4,369	4,552
Bookkeepers	5,273	5,176	4,298	4,544	4,684	4,369
Cashiers	3,404	3,087	3,228	3,165	3,346	4,345

Source: U.S., Department of Commerce, Census of the Population, 1970 (Washington, D.C., Government Printing Office, 1970), "Detailed Characteristics of Population (by State)", Tables 175, 177.

deteriorated for clerical workers in both absolute and relative terms: their unemployment rate had risen to 7.9 percent compared to 6.8 percent for all female white collar workers.[4] While clerical workers still experience lower unemployment rates than female blue collar workers, the level of unemployment among clerical workers contradicts the conventional wisdom.

Job security, established by holding a particular job for a long period, also seems to be disappearing for clerical workers. Technological changes in office equipment are simplifying the skills needed for many types of clerical work.[5] As a result, less experienced workers may be hired at lower wages to replace more experienced and well-paid employees. Under these conditions, the special skills that the experienced worker developed over the years no longer make her indispensable to the office. With new equipment, the same job can be learned relatively quickly by another worker. As a result, many clerical workers can be easily replaced as long as there is a large supply of available workers, a condition that is ensured by the pool of unemployed workers and the growth of the temporary help industry in clerical work.

Opportunity Gaps

A major obstacle to the advancement of women in the clerical work force is the fact that the field is surrounded by dead space; it lacks links to other areas in most employing organizations. Nonclerical jobs are given to outsiders who often receive on-the-job training, while clerical workers within the organization are rarely considered for these positions.

There are several different kinds of "opportunity gaps" in the clerical job market for women. The first gap exists at the entry level. Many women, especially those from minority groups, lack the basic clerical skills required to enable them to enter clerical jobs as an alternative to factory or service work (see Fig. 6.1). The woman who does have the basic skills for an entry level clerical job, like messenger, copy-machine operator, or file clerk, must somehow get over the second gap. She cannot move beyond these entry level jobs without

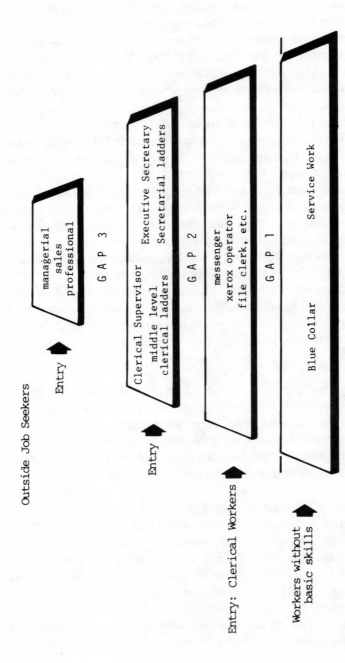

Figure 6.1 Opportunity gaps in clerical work: employment levels in hiring of clerical workers.

acquiring additional skills, but she can rarely obtain the needed training either on or through the job.

A third opportunity gap exists for the woman in higher level or skilled clerical jobs. She finds that her career ladder in terms of salary and status is limited. It is further limited by divisions between the secretarial ladder and other clerical positions. At the top of career ladders in the secretarial field are positions as executive secretaries or administrative assistants. At the top of most other clerical fields (for example, typist, or accounting clerk) is usually a supervisory position. Whichever position she is in, the woman at the top faces the most impenetrable barrier of all: that between clerical jobs and higher status, higher paying careers, such as sales, management, or semi-professional occupations.

The opportunity gaps are particularly wide in New England where a large pool of well-educated workers competes for available higher level positions. In Massachusetts, almost half of all women with high school diplomas and one out of six with college degrees end up as clerical workers. In the 1970s, the high unemployment in management and professional ranks made it particularly difficult for middle-level clerical workers to break through the third gap.

Quality of Work Life

In clerical work, the issue of quality of work is related to the issue of opportunity. Even if clerical workers were given open access to available higher level jobs, the number of such jobs is limited. Only a small number of presently employed clerical workers could be accommodated in higher positions. Thus the vast majority will necessarily remain in medium- or low-level clerical jobs. For them, the most important issue, aside from wages and job security, is the quality of work.

Judgments about quality of work are, of course, individual and subjective, but they typically involve such factors as the physical setting and comfort; the type, variety, and difficulty of job activities; the degree of supervision imposed on the worker; the range of skills that the workers can exercise; and the extent to which the workers can enjoy social relationships on the job.

Clerical work, traditionally performed in settings that are cleaner, safer, and quieter than blue collar work, has not been characterized by physical arduousness. Nevertheless, many quality of work problems exist.[6] These are particularly acute for women in large offices, such as those becoming more and more characteristic of huge financial and insurance company headquarters in Boston and Hartford. In many of these offices, clerical activities have been organized into small, standardized steps with automated systems and sophisticated office machinery to speed up work. Pools of workers or individual workers specialize in one set of small tasks, performing these limited activities repeatedly. Key punching is the most familiar example of this kind of job. These limited jobs are extremely boring and provide little challenge; they also fail to provide opportunities to develop and exercise skills. Workers in these jobs are usually closely supervised, isolated from other workers, and forced to sustain a tension-producing pace. These newer developments have removed one of the more attractive features of clerical work, the social give and take of the office.[7]

Most women clerical workers face a second set of problems in the more traditional smaller offices throughout the region. They are expected to perform a variety of services that are not part of the official definition of the job; for example, they often have to run personal errands, make and serve coffee, be deferential, serve as a scapegoat when things go wrong, and act as a target for sexual remarks.[8] Clerical workers are beginning to object to such personally degrading treatment, but the relative scarcity of jobs today renders this more difficult for individual women.

Some Explanations for Low Wages and Poor Conditions

Low wages and inadequate quality of work life persist because of the oversupply of women qualified for clerical work, termed by some economists as overcrowding. This is especially true in New England where more women work for pay and unemployment rates are higher than nationally. The oversupply is the result of an interaction of several factors.

First, the socialization of women tends to channel them

into family roles rather than into carefully selected work roles. Since clerical training is widely available, many accept tracking into clerical courses without serious consideration of alternative possibilities while they are in school. The result is that they have few other job skills and find clerical work the most accessible to them once they enter the job market.

Second, many educational institutions offer women little choice. Many public school vocational education programs seldom offer women students anything but clerical and personal service training. Career counseling for women students is stereotyped, narrowing rather than broadening their sense of what is possible.

Vocational programs sometimes forge ahead without examining the projections as to the numbers and types of jobs available. Graduates of the programs are rarely contacted to determine their success or failure. Many clerical programs, for example, stress stenography, which requires many hours of training; yet jobs using these skills are shrinking and typically pay less than other occupations that require fewer hours of training.

Third, when women enter the paid job market, they may discover that clerical jobs are the best among those open to them. Because of sex segregation in employment, the majority of the more attractive occupations have been and still are virtually closed to women. When the alternative options for women without college degrees are domestic service, waitressing, and saleswork, it is not surprising that many "choose" clerical work. Even for a growing number of recent college graduates, clerical work is frequently the only kind of job available. As noted above, a particularly large proportion of minority women with college degrees end up in clerical jobs (see Chapter 5).

Many problems of clerical workers are directly related to continuing high levels of unemployment. Women with qualifications in other fields, who are unable to find jobs, turn to clerical work, swelling the ranks of potential workers. This not only increases unemployment in the clerical category, but also enables employers to hire well-qualified workers at low wages. During periods of high unemployment, therefore, it is difficult for clerical workers to demand better wages or improved working conditions. Those who are troublesome can readily be replaced, especially when they are not organized. The high rates of unemployment also create divisions between groups of workers: old against young, white against black and other minorities, and so on. These divisions can be exploited to weaken efforts of workers to unite for better conditions.

The common myths about women have contributed significantly to the limited nature of clerical work and the absence of broader job opportunities. The characterization of clerical work as women's work may, in itself, be part of the explanation of low wages. There is considerable speculation that, as jobs become identified with women, employers find it easy to rationalize decisions to permit wages to lag and to neglect opportunities to upgrade or provide on-the-job training for female employees.

The belief that women are nurturing and helpful as encouraged both women clerical workers and their employers to collaborate in turning many clerical jobs into personal service jobs. Clerks sometimes become "office wives." Although women may not welcome this shift in job duties, the notion that they are supposed to be helpful makes it difficult for them to resist sex-typed extra work and pressures toward personalizing relationships.

Sex segregation within clerical occupations ensures that traditionally male jobs, which are higher paid relative to the skills required, remain closed to women, while large numbers of women compete for women's jobs. This creates overcrowding in the traditional women's jobs, which helps to keep wages low and jobs uncertain.

Most companies and government agencies have programs to encourage upward mobility. Generally, however, the programs are designed to identify a few highly motivated and/or exceptionally competent individuals who are "capable" of higher level work. "Bridge" jobs are often created to serve as training periods or apprenticeships for the higher level jobs (for example, assistant field investigator). However, these opportunities are usually directed at lower level administrators rather than at clerical workers, and the programs are small in relation to the total size of the work force. Since so few clerical workers are included in these upward mobility programs, the focus for the great majority should be on providing better jobs by job improvement or job enlargement.

Lack of Union Organization

All these factors combine with the attitudes and practices of male-dominated trade unions to leave clerical women as one of the least unionized of the major categories of workers. Past efforts to organize clerical workers have been inadequate. Unions, management, and others have assumed that this group is hard to organize because they are women, because they consider themselves semi-professionals rather than workers, and because they have close ties with their employers on the job. The relatively small effort established unions have put into organizing clericals suggests that unions need to learn more about clerical work and clerical workers.

Many clerical workers lack specific knowledge about the role of unions and the range of possible alternative workers' organizations. The absence of workers' organizations, like trade unions or occupational associations, has left women clericals with little or no collective strength in negotiations for wages, benefits, or job security.

The changing conditions of clerical work tend to make clerical workers riper for organizing than at any time in the past. The discussions among the women clerical workers at the workshop indicated that, especially in the larger "clerical factories" employing hundreds of women, there is a real desire to explore new ways of working together to improve their wages and security. At the same time, participants reported that women feared they might lose their jobs if they attempted to organize for collective bargaining. Some of the participants described the efforts of a new clerical workers' group, "9 to 5," which is trying to discover new ways of bringing clerical women together to overcome their fears and to provide them with collective bargaining tools in the New England area.

The Need for Legislation

Because clerical workers are usually not organized in unions, many workshop participants stressed that legislation is needed to protect and advance their welfare. They expressed concern that many clerical workers are unfamiliar with their rights under existing legislation. At the same time, they emphasized that many existing laws are inadequately enforced in relation to clerical workers. Laws and government agency policies determine the possibilities and limits for union organizing, for developing vocational programs, and for creating and maintaining on-the-job training programs. The participants suggested that special attention should be devoted to laws and rulings relating to issues like maternity leave, flexible work hours, and insurance for clerical workers. They maintained that the important issue in this area is not what kinds of *new* laws and policies are needed, but how *existing* laws and policies can be effectively enforced.

Service Workers

Rapidly Expanding Numbers

Next to clerical work, the largest number of women in New England today work in the service category. This encompasses a wide variety of jobs including FBI agent, police officer, beauty operator, and janitor. A growing population, expanding business activity, increasing leisure time, and rising levels of disposable personal income have created a rapidly expanding demand for service workers in recent decades.

Nationally, the rate of expanding employment in this category is expected to slow down between 1975 and 1985 to a rate somewhat lower than that projected for overall employment. This is primarily because the employment of household workers, almost one out of five women in service jobs, is expected to decline from 1.4 to 1.1 million. When they are excluded, the service worker category is expected to expand at a rate of 29 percent, somewhat faster than total employment.

The Lowest Wages of All

Despite the rapid growth in employment, the median wages of both men and women in the services are the lowest of all the major job categories. The wages of women service workers are little more than half those of men. Only slightly over 15 percent of all service workers earned more than $10,000 in 1970, a year when the Bureau of Labor Statistics estimated that an urban family of four needed $10,087 to live in moderate circumstances.

Table 7.1

Percentage of Women, Blacks, and Hispanic Workers among All New England
Service Workers in 1970

State	Total Number of Service Workers	Percent Women	Percent Black	Percent Hispanic
Connecticut	121,885	51.0	18.5	12.7
Maine	39,875	57.3	22.1	21.7
Massachusetts	272,915	50.2	21.0	3.2
New Hampshire	35,464	71.6	(a)	(a)
Rhode Island	44,941	51.4	36.2	11.8
Vermont	23,616	74.5	(a)	(a)

Source: U.S., Department of Commerce, Census of the Population, 1970
(Washington, D.C., Government Printing Office, 1970), "Characteristics of
Population (by State)", Table 54.

Note: ᵃInsignificant percentage of families.

Not all service jobs are poorly paid. A few service workers, like detectives, receive fairly high salaries. But there are
almost no women in these jobs. In every state in New
England, women are concentrated in the lower paid food and
health services and private household work. Their median
wages are only 55 to 57 percent of men's.

Blacks and other minorities constitute a higher proportion of women employed in service work than in any other
category in New England. Black women make up 17.8 percent of all women service workers in the region, although
they constitute only about 3 percent of the regional population (see Table 7.1). In private household service, the only
job in which women constitute over 95 percent of all wage
earners, black women make up a little over half (53 percent)
of the total female work force.

The marginal status of women service workers is illustrated not only by their relegation to lower paying jobs, but
also by their higher rates of unemployment than men in these

occupations. Many women, as well as minority men, tend to become especially discouraged by the low pay and poor conditions prevalent in most service work. The 1970 census data showed that about 10,000 service workers were unemployed in Massachusetts, a little more than half of them women. But about twelve times that number (127,000) were reported to have dropped out of the paid labor force, having last worked during the 1960s. This equals almost half the number of employed service workers. About two-thirds of these were women.

Research during the war on poverty led to the discovery that 22 percent of those whom the government defined as poor were working full-time at low paying jobs, a high proportion of them in service work.[1] This contradicts the popular notion that a job leads one out of poverty and highlights the need to help workers in this category to qualify for higher paying employment. The 1970 *Manpower Report of the President* proposed a national upgrading program[2] to (1) improve workers' job skills and their ability to cope with the environmental problems that affect work capability, and (2) enable workers in a reasonably brief period to increase their earnings through advancement to higher paid jobs and more stable employment. These proposals have yet to be put into effect in most service jobs. In the booming field of personal service, for example, most minority women never advance beyond the status of hairdresser. Only one out of a hundred will succeed in becoming a shop manager.

One of the characteristics of service work is its fragmentation into different job markets. There is no clear line of promotion or upgrading for individuals within and certainly not between these separate markets.

Private Household Workers

The plight of private household workers in the North was brought to national attention by several national black women's organizations and the National Association for the Advancement of Colored People (NAACP) in the early 1960s, when many girls and women were migrating from the South and looking for jobs. These workers receive the lowest pay and are perceived as having the lowest status of all employees in the service category.

As the workshop participants emphasized, household workers often must have many skills, including an ability to take care of children, sick and elderly persons, as well as to handle increasingly complex household machinery. They must assume the reponsibility for running the household when the owners are away.

Yet little attention is paid to improving the income and conditions of household workers. Workshop participants pointed out that some middle-income women who have obtained paid jobs seek to pay as low wages as possible to those who care for their homes and families. Household workers are typically expected to work long hours, often at inconvenient times. They do not receive workmen's compensation in many states. Both they and their employers often ignore federal laws requiring social security payments; the former do so because they cannot afford any reduction in their already-too-low income, and the latter because they wish to avoid any additional payments. Since there is no effective system of inspecting the wages and working conditions of most household workers, they typically end up, after many years of work, without any recourse to social security in their old age.

Most women employed in household work fall into one of two age brackets: 18 to 25, before they marry and have children; and 45 to 60, after their children have grown and they need to earn additional income for family or personal needs. They typically lack other job skills. Many are welfare recipients, making "private" arrangements for a little extra work to augment their inadequate welfare payments. This makes them especially reluctant to seek outside help to improve their conditions because welfare legislation in most states provides that women on welfare who earn any wages must deduct an equivalent amount from their welfare payments.

There are few ways in which the household employee, working by herself for an individual employer, can improve her conditions or wages. Her employer may, at any time, arbitrarily terminate her job. There is little incentive for her to improve her skills through added training, for there is no way to require her employer to pay her more for those improvements. If she seeks to obtain a better job elsewhere, she must rely on her former employer's good will for a recommendation. There is no recognized outside licensing agency that can certify that she has acquired specific skills and is qualified for a better paying, more responsible kind of work.

One potential avenue for increasing the productivity and incomes of houseworkers is through housecleaning and servicing companies, which provide complete and mechanized services by groups of people working cooperatively. Housecleaning and servicing companies of this type are, however, for the most part run primarily by men amd mainly employ men; women have been excluded. If women could be organized into cooperatives to undertake the provision of these types of services, they might be able to improve their incomes from this type of employment. Few attempts have been made to involve women in New England in this type of program.

All these features of household employment combined have rendered women who take these kinds of jobs among the most marginal of all workers. There are few opportunities for them, if they are laid off, to obtain jobs in other, more skilled categories. Thus, they are easy prey to employment agencies, which help them find jobs in return for deducting a percentage from their already too-low wages.

It is unfortunate that more research has not been done to expose the characteristics of household work and the problems confronting those who work in the industry. They are among the most exploited members of society. In a sense, too, they are the most immediate victims of the changing division of labor by which an increasing share of household work is being taken over by outside industry. Higher income women may decide either to hire them and/or to buy new household machinery, prepared foods, and so forth, to reduce their own burden of household work. The household worker who works in others' homes has no choice. She must work to earn money. Yet she receives so little in wages that she is frequently forced to leave her own children and home inadequately cared for. As household employment declines in the coming decades, with the increased introduction of labor-saving devices, these women are likely (unless new skills and other jobs are made available to them) to find themselves once again dependent on inadequate welfare payments.

In New England, a number of organizations have sought to improve the status of private household workers. The Women's Service Club of Boston, an affiliate of the National Association of Colored Women's Club, Inc., has a nine-year-old program to protect the household worker. The service club established a homemaker training program, which certified 400 women who completed a twelve-week course, thus improving their skills as household workers. The service club also established the Massachusetts Committee on Household Employment consisting of 27 community, private, and public organizations concerned with upgrading the status of household workers. Funded through the Office of Economic Opportunity of the Department of Health, Education, and Welfare and the Department of Labor, it is affiliated with the National Committee on Household Employment.

The national committee was founded in 1964 by a group of concerned public service organizations and individuals. Its first major program, funded by the Department of Labor, was the establishment of eight experimental projects in different states. These projects tested various methods of recruiting, training, counseling, and placing household workers. The Massachusetts Committee on Household Employment, a training program set up in 1968, is still operating one of the eight experimental demonstration programs. The national committee also established a code of standards to protect the rights of household workers and to provide guidelines for structuring their work situations.

The Massachusetts committee has been working with the national committee to improve legislation affecting household workers. It concentrated on a state law to include domestic workers under state labor legislation that was passed on August 24, 1970. Under the law, (1) powers of enforcement were given to the Division of Labor and Industries,

(2) Chapter 150A gave household workers the right to unionize, and (3) Chapter 151 provided minimum wage rates to domestics linked to the general minimum wage for all other workers. This is the first law in the country to provide minimum wages for household workers.

The national and Massachusetts committees are working for passage of national and state laws to provide insurance benefits for household workers. The Massachusetts committee has proposed legislation to protect household workers and part-time domestic employees under the Massachusetts Workmen's Compensation Laws. The legislative committee of the national committee has met with insurance companies to study the feasibility of covering household workers under homeowner policies.

The national committee's legislative task force has been conferring, too, with federal administrators about licensing household workers to certify their skills and thus establish some credentials and criteria for upward mobility. One difficulty comes from many household workers who do not wish their occupation to be known. This is partly because of its present stigma and partly because, under existing laws, they might lose their welfare benefits, which are essential to supplement their low wages.

The Health Service

Unlike private household work, health service is a booming industry. Employment is expanding, mainly because of a national trend toward preventive medicine. Nationally, annual total expenditures on health service are likely to exceed $70 billion by the end of the 1970s. Employment has doubled in the past ten years, and the field provides a wide variety of job opportunities.

A large majority of health workers are employed in hospitals. Others work in nursing homes, private offices, clinics, laboratories, and related institutions.

Women in the health services, as in other fields, are nevertheless concentrated in the lower level positions. They are far less likely than men to be recruited into the more prestigious, better paid occupations.

The institutional barriers to the advancement of women into more skilled, higher paying posts are qualitatively different in the health service field than in private household work. The situation in hospitals, where a large percentage of female health service workers are employed, can serve as an illustration. A rigid occupational structure hinders horizontal mobility in most hospitals. A food service supervisor, for example, cannot become a nursing supervisor. At the same time, vertical mobility is limited by formal job requirements set by professional organizations and enforced by state and local licensing statutes as well as by hospital accreditation procedures. The departmental opportunity for nurse aides, who require no special skills or training, are far more limited than for nurses. There are no direct promotion possibilities based on skills acquired on the job. They cannot typically become nurses without leaving their jobs to attend school. Yet this may constitute a serious barrier for a woman who may wish, after some years of experience, to improve her status. She is usually working because of personal or family need and cannot afford to take time off from her paid work to acquire the necessary qualifications.

A similar barrier exists for women employed in medical laboratories. Laboratory assistants are usually required to have a high school diploma, but need no special training beyond that. Technicians must either have completed a two-year training program approved by the city or state, or they must pass an examination. Assistants may qualify as technicians by taking an examination. Job experience alone is usually not enough to pass the exam. They must typically obtain classroom instruction, which requires leaving work for a period of time—which, again, few women can afford to do.

Food service departments account for about one out of every ten hospital employees. Dietary aides are at the bottom of the occupational structure. These positions have no special entry requirement. Food service supervisors, in contrast, usually must have a high school diploma and some specialized training or related experience, and they receive a slightly higher salary. Like the nurse aide and lab assistant, however, the woman dietary aide who wishes to improve her position must typically leave her job to obtain the necessary credentials.

Some health service training programs have been provided in New England in recent years, but more needs to be done to enable the low-paid health service workers to take advantage of them, and they need to be made available to more women.

Many major health career programs for hospital workers have been funded locally through Title I monies. In Massachusetts, for example, a variety of institutions are providing training for health personnel. Northeastern University in Boston awards an associate arts degree for its two-year family worker program. Boston University has a similar program to train mental health aides. Another program, Opening the Doors Wider in Nursing (ODWIN), has existed for almost ten years.

Massachusetts has had a Health Vocational Training Program since 1970. Out of 450 persons trained, 390 were women. Trainees receive stipends, and the programs include training for four health-related jobs.

1. Nursing Assistant (fifteen-week course; certificate received). Most graduates are assigned to a health center, where they are only allowed to take temperatures and blood pressure and make beds. Trainees are counseled about their ability to pursue a L.P.N., R.N., or B.S. in nursing. Many students have gone on for further training, but most cannot afford to or do not have the desire. Credits are not transferable.
2. Medical Transcriber or Secretary (six-month course; certificate received). The career option and pay scale are higher than for nursing assistants.
3. Operating Room Technician (forty-eight-week course). Both career options and pay scale are higher, and graduates are certified by the American Medical Association.
4. Respiratory Therapy Technician (one-year course; certified by the American Medical Association). Relatively few women take the course, considering the number

of women in the health field. Seventeen women, only four of whom were black, completed the course out of a total of forty persons in 1975. After all this training it is still very difficult to get into the technicians' union.

In New England, hospitals themselves have become important training institutions, providing on-the-job training for all newly hired nurse aides, dietary aides, and laboratory aides. The problem is that Medicaid overseers will only reimburse people or centers that have administrative staff with master's degrees. This excludes most of the health centers that have been established in recent years by participation of community groups.

The overriding difficulty remains, however, that many women are unable to leave their jobs to take the full-time courses offered. Nor is it easy, without outside assistance, to manage a full-time job, a full course, and family responsibilities. Even part-time courses are difficult for them to manage. But there are almost no part-time courses or complete on-the-job training programs to substitute for the full-time programs.

The Food Service Industry

The food service industry, the largest employer of woman service workers, offers women less upward mobility than the health services. The majority of workers in the field are employed by restaurants and bars. Another sizable group works in hotel-restaurants. Finally, there is a large group, estimated at over half a million nationally, engaged in food service operations in large institutions like schools, hospitals, and prisons.

Entry into and mobility within the food industry can be through three broad employment channels: dining room, kitchen, and managerial. Almost all the positions in the dining room category (waitress and waiter, busboy, and counterperson) are entry level jobs. Educational requirements are minimal. Waitresses and waiters may have to read a menu and add a bill, but cafeteria workers or busboys do not even need these skills. In almost every case, new employees receive whatever brief training is needed from the firm.

Once on the job, there is little occupational mobility within the dining room. Occasionally a busboy may be promoted to a waiter. Waitresses and waiters can usually improve their status only by making new contacts and moving into openings at higher-priced restaurants where tips are greater.

Some potential mobility exists in the kitchen and food preparation employment cluster, the second largest food service group. Porters and dishwashers are paid low wages, but in some establishments they receive a free meal. The job requires no special skills and is easy to learn in a very short time. The methods currently used to train cooks, however, do not produce a satisfactory number of adequately prepared candidates. The pattern of informal training by observation and worker-programmed instruction contributes to the high turnover and low productivity that characterize the industry. Mobility is achieved by moving on to another job involving heavier responsibility, more skill, or better pay and/or working conditions. On-the-job training can be supplemented by formal institutional instruction in the culinary arts (for example, baking and meat cutting). The courses are not standard and the trainee must piece together a curriculum from a variety of different schools. Individuals program their own on-the-job training, and personal initiative is important in upgrading.

Employers of salaried managers, the third food service group, seek individuals with more than a high school education. The industry typically prefers college graduates in business administration or in special programs in hotel and restaurant management. Because the industry is low paying and not very glamorous, managers are difficult to recruit. Some junior college graduates or those with some college experience may be hired as assistant managers or management trainees.

Women are mainly employed in the lowest income levels in the food industry. To a large degree this is because of their concentration in waitress positions, which frequently are part-time, low-wage jobs. Women have little prospect for increased earnings because most high-price restaurants use waiters rather than waitresses, and females are not recruited or promoted to higher-salaried kitchen or management positions. Consequently, few women are able to move up into better paying jobs.

Blacks and Hispanic personnel are disproportionately represented in almost all except the highest paying jobs. It appears that they may move into all kitchen and dining room jobs, but they are not hired as managers or supervisors.

Blue Collar Workers

The Relative Decline in Blue Collar Jobs

The blue collar work force is made up of skilled crafts-persons and kindred workers, factory operatives, and non-farm laborers. In the mature industrial New England economy, 1.8 million workers, about 38 percent of all men and women in the paid work force, are employed in these kinds of jobs. This is slightly higher than the national average of 36 percent. In New England, a significantly higher proportion of women (22 percent) work in these categories than nationally (17 percent).

Statistics (see Table 8.1) show that women are still largely excluded from skilled crafts. Nationally, the proportion of women has only barely inched up in the last ten years from 3 percent to 5 percent of all workers holding skilled jobs. In New England, the proportion is slightly larger, about 7 percent.

In the most industrialized New England state, Massachusetts (where almost half of all blue collar workers in the region are employed), women constitute about a quarter of these workers. Projections for blue collar employment in New England are not optimistic. In Massachusetts, employment in only a few industries has increased: employment in the durable products sector (furniture, machinery, and steel) and in hard goods (for example, transport, equipment, ship-building), both starting on a small base, grew 14 and 89 percent, respectively. Overall, in contrast, the number of men in blue collar work dropped by 30,000 while that of women

Table 8.1

New England Blue Collar Work Force in 1970

	Massachusetts	Connecticut	Rhode Island	Maine	New Hampshire	Vermont	New England
Total Blue Collar Workers	814,195	466,756	163,058	166,804	124,927	57,629	1,793,369
% of total work force	35	37	43	45	50	36	38
% of New England blue collar force	45	26	9	9	7	3	100
Total Women in Blue Collar Jobs	185,002	100,500	47,590	39,802	32,677	8,057	413,628
% of blue collar workers	23	22	29	24	26	13	23
% of women workers	20	21	31	29	29	13	22
% of skilled category	7	6	9	6	6	5	7
% of operatives and laborers	33	33	40	33	41	20	33

Source: Calculated from U. S., Department of Commerce, Census of the Population, 1970 (Washington, D.C., Government Printing Office, 1970), "Characteristics of Population (by State)", Table 54.

declined by 10,000 in the decade of the 1960s. Much of the decrease was due to the steady decline in the traditional, relatively labor-intensive industries like textiles, leather, and shoes. Projected openings for 1980 are in the skilled operative jobs and due to death and retirement rather than industrial growth. Only in the northern tier states, Vermont and New Hampshire, where wages are lower, has blue collar employment increased.

There are several possible reasons for the higher proportion of women working in blue collar jobs in New England than nationally. It may be that a higher proportion of low income, unskilled women must work for pay in the region than nationally, and these are the only jobs for which they qualify.[1] Employers and employees in New England may have a more ready acceptance of women blue collar workers because of their long history in the textile industry; female participation in the early days of the industry was accepted because the work was considered closely allied to home activities.

Historically, in New England as elsewhere, the blue collar market had expanded primarily for men, with only the low-level, low-paying jobs being reserved for women except in peak employment periods, such as during World Wars I and II. The greater decline in blue collar jobs for men than women in the recent period in Massachusetts appears to reflect the shifting overall structure of the regional economy. Increased mechanization and the reduction of skilled jobs in New England has been accompanied by the creation of lower paid, less skilled jobs for which increasing numbers of women have been hired. At the same time, many labor-intensive jobs have been lost to the lower wage areas of the northern tier states, the southern sun belt, and even overseas. These trends warrant further research.

Census data for the three most industrialized New England states show that black and Spanish-speaking women are significantly more likely to find jobs in the less desirable operative category than elsewhere. The educational qualifications of the minority workers in these industries appear to be higher than those of other women. White and Spanish-

Table 8.2

Median Blue Collar Wages for Women and Men in New England, 1970

	Median Blue Collar Wage	Median Women's Wage	Median Men's Wage	Median Women's Wage as Percentage of Median Men's Wage
Massachusetts	$4,811	$3,148	$6,474	49
Connecticut	5,453	4,021	6,885	58
Rhode Island	4,103	3,144	5,063	62
Maine	4,120	2,970	5,271	56
New Hampshire	4,501	3,020	6,001	50
Vermont	4,296	3,123	5,469	57
New England	4,547	3,238	5,856	55

Source: U. S., Department of Commerce, Census of Population, 1970 (Washington, D.C., Government Printing Office, 1970), "Characteristics of Population (by State)", Tables 175, 176.

speaking women with less than three years of high school seem more likely than black women to be able to obtain operative jobs.

A far higher proportion of black women with that much education are to be found in the still lower paying service and private household occupations.

Low Wages

Women's wages in blue collar work, except in Massachusetts, are little more than half men's (see Table 8.2). This reflects the fact that, although a higher proportion of women enter blue collar work in New England than elsewhere, they are confined for the most part, as in the rest of the country, to the lowest paying jobs as assemblers, checkers, packers, sewers, and stitchers. Men are electricians, carpenters, machinists, shipfitters, and tailors. The median earnings for women who do obtain crafts jobs are about $3,000 less than men's, while they are about $2,000 less in operative jobs.

In Massachusetts, women's median earnings are $3,148, less than half the median earnings of men. Part of this larger than average wage differential arises from the fact that a far higher proportion of men than women are employed in the higher-paying construction, transport, communications, and public utilities jobs. About four-fifths of all women blue collar workers are concentrated in manufacturing, where their earnings are a little over half (57 percent) of men's.

The Range of Explanations

Little research has been done on blue collar work in general (except for time and motion studies), and almost none has been done on women in blue collar work. Most of the useful research was done between 1900 and 1925. Until 1975, researchers had not devoted a single book to women employed in blue collar jobs. Of the 559 papers included in the *Industrial Relations Research Association Proceedings* between 1966 and 1972, none dealt primarily with women. Lack of research makes it more difficult to change employer-employee practices, since myths rationalizing them persist unchallenged.

Socialization of women specifically discourages most women from obtaining the kinds of skills required to obtain higher paying blue collar jobs: little girls are seldom invited to work with their fathers fixing cars; elementary textbooks never picture women in skilled crafts jobs; mothers and fathers reinforce the idea that women cannot do mechanical things.

Both male and female blue collar workers are, today, expressing growing dissatisfaction and feelings of alienation. This has been documented by the Department of Health, Education, and Welfare's Special Task Force on Work in America.[2] Families are unlikely to encourage women to move out of dull, uninteresting "female" jobs into those that are already recognized as bad work environments for men.

Occupational health and safety are closely related problems of concern for all workers, but with specific implications for women, both in blue collar jobs they may now hold and in nontraditional jobs known to be hazardous for the health of men. Pregnant women may be especially vulnerable. More research is needed in this area.

Obstacles appear to block the advance of women into more skilled types of blue collar work in four major areas: corporate hiring and upgrading practices, union policies, apprenticeship programs, and vocational education.

Corporate Hiring and Upgrading Practices

Employer recruiting, testing, and training for blue collar jobs has been limited by uncritical acceptance of myths about the inherent differences in technical aptitude between men and women. Although there has been relatively little research in this area, what has been done shows no significant sex differences. Yet women still have been almost automatically put on unskilled, low-paid, assembly line jobs. The persistence of the myth that women work only for pin money reinforces negative attitudes of blue collar working men, as well as managers, toward women taking more skilled jobs which might pay more.

It has been argued that protective legislation, particularly laws relating to weight lifting and overtime requirements, has tended to reduce the demand for women in blue collar work, especially in the more physically demanding jobs. Women workshop participants pointed out that, despite such laws, women have not infrequently been employed at dull and physically unpleasant jobs that are technically difficult. Their pay has seldom been commensurately increased.

Companies have come under a degree of legal pressure today to achieve equal employment opportunities through government contracts, consent decrees, and compliance agreements. Several companies in New England indicate their willingness to share their experiences with affirmative action programs. Representatives described their programs at the workshops. The programs consist primarily of incorporating women in training programs formerly limited primarily to men and encouraging women to take on some nontraditional blue collar jobs.

Some company spokespersons reported difficulties in recruiting women into their programs initially until a number were involved. Some asserted that women did not want to take on heavy jobs, like changing tires in auto repair shops.

Women heads of families seemed more willing to put up with possible objections of fellow workers because they wanted the higher wages the new jobs would bring them. Other employer representatives explained that, with educational programs among the workers, they had been able to bring a number of women into new programs and even to promote them to more senior and even supervisory positions.

A number of workshop participants argued, however, that too many of the available reports on the effects of affirmative action have come from employers; women affected by these programs need to be heard. When affirmative action leads to placing a few women among male workers, the men tend to complain. They maintain they have to lift heavy things for women, which interferes with their own work. Many women are unenthusiastic about being isolated among male workers. Their own socialization, as well as peer and family attitudes, may exert pressures on them to prefer working with other women. The fact that other jobs have not been opened to them in the past may also influence their preferences.

The workshop participants suggested that, since decisions to place women among men are often made without discussion, "from the top down," the workers and lower level managers do not understand the reasons and give little support for the programs. If the women fail, the employer then says, "See, I tried, and it doesn't work." As Robert Ackerman has emphasized, "Edicts from on high and staff activity don't effect any change; it has to be 'institutionalized' in the operating units."[3]

Some workshop participants pointed out that affimative action places too much emphasis on getting a few women into nontraditional jobs, rather than on improving the quality of work in "female jobs" where most women are currently and probably will be employed for some time. Following the description by a personnel manager of the successful recruitment of 14 women into a training program for mechanics involving about 145 persons, a woman at the workshop commented that several thousands of women, who work on the assembly lines of the same firm, continue to receive relatively low pay. Hundreds had been laid off at the time the 14 women were being upgraded. The job perspectives of these far larger numbers of women would remain unaltered even if twice as many women had been recruited into the training program.

At the same time, the workshop participants emphasized the importance of effective enforcement of legislation providing for equal opportunities and affirmative action. Although women in these jobs have initiated complaints and lawsuits, the costs have been high. For many women, their marginal employment status and low incomes make them feel it is too risky to undertake any individual initiatives which may endanger their existing jobs. All too often, however, they are not even aware of their rights under the law.

Trade Unionism

Samuel Gompers, the founder of the American Federation of Labor, declared, in 1912, "Organizing women is not an act of charity."[4] The workshop participants claimed it is, if anything, more true today that women constitute a potential resource for new members, new leaders, and new issues to strengthen effective collective bargaining, especially in blue collar work. Yet male union members still tend to resist organizing women and accepting them in jobs and leadership positions. This is especially true in the skilled trades.

Almost half of the women in blue collar work in New England are organized in unions; this is a far higher proportion than among women workers in general (see Table 8.3). Yet the percentage of women blue collar workers in unions, even in New England, declined sharply from 54 to 44 percent from 1960 to 1970. Those who are organized are concentrated in a very few unions, over half of them in twelve labor organizations. One factor contributing to the decline of women union membership in New England has been the fact that the textile and shoe industries, in both of which women were relatively well organized, have been moving out of the area.

Unions have had both positive and negative effects on women's employment opportunities. Some unions have filed

Table 8.3
Union Membership of Men and Women as Percentage of all Workers in the Northeast and in the Nation

A. In the Northeast

	Men in Unions (%)			Women in Unions (%)		
	1960	1970	% Change	1960	1970	% Change
Total (All Workers)[a]	36	35	- 1	22	20	- 2
Blue collar workers	55	54	- 1	54	44	-10
Operatives & kindred	60	59	- 1	57	46	-11

B. In the Nation in each Industry in 1970

	Men in Unions (%)				Women in Unions (%)			
	Total	Manufact.	Trans/Comm Pub. Utilities	Retail	Total	Manufact.	Trans/Comm Pub. Utilities	Retail
Total (All Workers)[b]	28	38	49	13	10	23	29	7
Blue collar workers	42	50	59	18	28	32	13	14
Operatives & kindred	46	54	58	18	29	32	11	17

Source: U. S., Department of Labor, Bureau of Labor Statistics, Monthly Labor Review, "Women in Unions", May 1974.

Notes: [a]Year-round, full-time private wage and salary workers
[b]Private wage and salary workers

complaints of discrimination by employers on behalf of their female members. A Connecticut woman working with the AFL-CIO political action program described how affirmative action and equal employment opportunity guidelines and programs have begun, increasingly, to be negotiated as part of collective bargaining agreements. Union grievance procedures offer an alternative, and, in some cases, a quicker way of resolving discrimination compaints than taking individual initiative to utilize the complex equal employment act enforcement machinery.

In some instances, however, unions have actually hindered women from improving their job status. Some union men have expressed fears that affirmative action for women and minorities threatens their own hard-won seniority status. Some unions and companies have been charged with discrimination under Title VIII of the 1964 Civil Rights Act, and collective bargaining agreements have sometimes had to be changed to ensure equal opportunity. Under the consent decree affecting AT&T, for example, the International Brotherhood of Electrical Workers has had to renegotiate the contract as it affected women workers to ensure they received equal treatment.

A major study of women trade union members in New York City[5] showed that rank and file women tend to be more active than men in voting, attending meetings, participating in social and educational events, and filing grievances. Their participation is likely to be higher and acceptance greater, however, where there are more other women in the union. The study also showed that women in unions are more likely to be the sole support of their families than nonunion women and are less likely to have interrupted their pattern of work life for family reasons.

The study identified a number of factors that hinder women from achieving active leadership positions in unions. These include lack of successful role models and support by the male hierarchy, a tendency of job supervisors to give women activists a hard time, and the common attitude among men and women that women should be helpers rather than leaders. Home responsibilities and their husbands' objections to outside activities tended to limit some women's participation. These obstacles, the authors of the study suggested, might be overcome if unions tried harder to convince their male members of the necessity of involving women more effectively in collective bargaining for the benefit of all workers.

The workshop participants noted that similar difficulties block women's participation in unions in New England. Male union leaders tend to lack sensitivity to the special difficulties women confront in assuming leadership. A woman international union organizer, for example, was assigned to organize male workers in a shop on the opposite side of the state from her home, despite the fact that she had small children. This not only caused her great personal hardship, but did not appear to be an optimal use of her ability from the union's point of view.

The workshop discussions indicated that New England unions had done relatively little to promote minority women as members and far less into leadership. This appeared to be reflected in the remarks of the minority participants who seemed to expect little assistance from unions in improving the status of black or other minority women workers, although some of them were working with unions to place minority women in apprenticeship programs.

Union women nationally have begun various kinds of actions to improve their position. The Coalition of Labor Union Women (CLUW) was established nationally in 1974, and the first meeting involved over 3,000 women trade unionists. The organization has received strong support from a number of national unions as well as women's groups. It is now trying to organize on a local level, and has begun to form New England chapters.

Some national unions, like the United Auto Workers, have created women's departments. Others, like the International Union of Electrical Workers, have their own union affirmative action program.

Another type of activity is the Trade Union Women's Studies Program, which provides counseling programs for trade union women, as well as courses on grievance handling, labor history, and leadership training. The program is currently being expanded in New York state and includes an evaluation component.

Apprenticeship

Apprenticeship has long been a major mobility channel for less well-educated male workers. Apprenticeship programs are run primarily by employers or by unions through joint apprenticeship committees in construction and other trades. Most programs are approved and monitored by federal and/or state apprenticeship bureaus, but they are almost exclusively staffed by men from the apprentice trades.

Women have usually been excluded from apprenticeship programs except in a few traditionally female fields like cosmetology. Most traditionally female jobs are considered inappropriate for apprenticeship programs on the grounds that they are too unskilled to require prolonged training. Negative attitudes about women's lack of technical ability have carried over to hinder application of new governmental rulings to open up more skilled jobs to them. Even in recent years, for example, the Office of Federal Contract Compliance has excluded women from goals and timetables for affirmative action for minorities in hometown plans for the construction industry. The Bureau of Apprenticeship and Trainings's affirmative action plans for the trades, similarly, cover minorities, but not women.

The Directory of Occupational Titles tends to underrate a number of traditionally female jobs that could be apprenticeable trades. This document, prepared by the Department of Labor, defines some 22,000 occupations in more than 230 industries. It is the basis on which many public and private agencies evaluate prerequisites, career ladder criteria, and position in the classification and compensation hierarchies of large organizations.

In general, the workshop discussions reaffirmed the results of a study done in Wisconsin[6] that found that absence of women from apprenticeship programs was not due to women's unwillingness to do particular kinds of work. In some places, women are already doing what is often considered unsuitable work involving heavy, dirty jobs, being out in all weather, and handling dangerously hot materials. They are excluded, nevertheless, from the higher paying more attractive jobs because of lack of apprenticeship opportunities.

Some workshop participants noted that employers seemed to exhibit less bias against giving women more responsibility when they are working in nontraditional jobs. This may reflect the fact that, once the employer has decided to give women a break, he has already rejected the stereotype that might previously have hindered him from letting her advance. Or it may be that an affirmative action employer is one who was less convinced of the myth of female inferiority in the first place.

The workshop discussions indicated that in New England, as in Wisconsin, several barriers hinder women from becoming apprentices:

1. Many apprentice programs limit the maximum age of entrance, usually to twenty-seven years old. Young girls may anticipate only a short work experience before marrying and raising a family, so they are unwilling to enter apprenticeship programs. Later when they come to realize their value, it may be too late. Many women, who would like to enter apprenticeship programs after their children are in school, or who find themselves as single parents supporting themselves and their children, are excluded by this maximum age provision.
2. Veterans' preferences give men an advantage over women. A veteran, typically a man, is automatically given priority for the limited openings available in apprenticeship programs.
3. Internal programs, run by employers, or joint apprenticeship programs may recruit from vocational training schools or the shop floor where women seldom are employed. Women may not know how to apply for admission. High school counselors often lack information about apprenticeship possibilities, especially for women.

4. Attitudes of employers and unions in manpower training and placement programs often work to exclude
women.

The Wisconsin project concluded that more attention
should be focused on (1) improving employer attitudes
toward female apprentices, (2) making day-care work apprenticeships more feasible, (3) improving internal company
programs in periods of economic slack, and (4) redesigning
the Directory of Occupational Titles. In 1977, three programs were successfully functioning as pilot projects in six
cities, including Boston, where they are run by the Recruitment and Training Program, Inc. (RTP) and Nontraditional
Jobs for Women at the Boston YWCA.

The two Boston programs work with employers and
unions to train and place women as carpenters, electricians,
and builders. Some progress has been made, but unemployment in the building trades has been particularly severe in
Boston—rising as high as 40 percent—which has hindered the
training and placement of any new workers. Experiences in
other parts of the country indicate that in conditions of full
employment these programs can be successful.

Vocational Education

Vocational education is a growing field, both nationally
and in New England. Enrollments and funding have been increasing significantly in recent years. There is evidence, however, that it has not benefited even men as much as the expansion would seem to suggest. Less than a fourth of male
vocational education graduates are placed in related jobs by
the schools from which they graduate.

New England workshop participants who were closely involved with vocational education programs cited example
after example of their lack of relevance to the real work
world. In some instances, the equipment used in the teaching
program was outmoded. In others the equipment was too advanced, as in the case of fancy tools for testing automobile
fitness, which few garages actually own. In both cases,
graduates have to learn other more relevant skills to hold a

job in the field. Too often, the education they receive fails to provide them with the necessary background information and problem-solving skills required to adapt to the work situations they actually encounter.

These generally recognized weaknesses of vocational educational programs, workshop participants claimed, are combined with a failure to meet the needs of women in particular. Women constitute over half of all vocational school students, but most of them are relegated to traditional female areas—and these do not include skilled blue collar jobs. Almost no women hold leadership positions in advisory councils or as state directors, administrators, or instructors. Minority women may be segregated in schools and placement, benefiting even less than white women from the programs.

Yet research shows that women are potentially as capable as men in every important blue collar skill. There are almost no significant sex differences in major aptitude and knowledge areas. Where differences do exist, men excel in two and women in four of the areas tested.[7] As Jack Willars has declared, "Vocational programs must be destereotyped from top to bottom."[8]

Some current activities to improve vocational education in New England include the involvement of girls in an introductory building trades course (at Exeter High School in New Hampshire) and a program to coordinate high school programs and industrial needs in sciences and technology by bringing together vocational educators and corporations (at the Massachusetts Institute of Technology). Massachusetts State Law 622 now provides equal educational opportunities for girls in vocational education, although its implementation needs to be evaluated. These programs are only a beginning. Much more needs to be done.

The Professions

More Skilled, Higher Paid, But . . .

Women professionals are more skilled and qualified for a range of higher paid, more attractive kinds of work than most women. But the persistence of an ideology that would assign women primarily to familial roles has fostered the institution-alization of education, hiring, and upgrading practices which leave even professional women in lower paid jobs with less responsibility and likelihood of advancement than similarly qualified men. In teaching and nursing, which are particularly perceived as allied to their anticipated family role, women have come to provide a readily available, relatively low cost labor reserve.

The census category of Professional, Technical, and Kindred Workers (PTK) covers a heterogeneous group of oc-cupations, employing 60.5 percent of women and 66.1 per-cent of men who have attained four or more years of college. For simplicity, these occupations are included here together under the rubric, the professions. The status of women in the professions, it might be noted, has received more attention in terms of research than any other employment category, per-haps because researchers doing most of this work have been so personally concerned.

In New England, professional employment provides a slightly higher proportion (16.7 percent) of all jobs available to women than throughout the nation (15.7 percent). More than two-thirds of all professional women in the region are employed in Massachusetts and Connecticut where they compose a still higher proportion of all women workers (over 17 percent). This appears to reflect the fact that, as specialization has spread throughout the world over the last century, Connecticut and Massachusetts have remained among the nation's leading financial and distributive centers. At the same time, Massachusetts, in particular, has become the home of more institutions of higher learning and research than any other single state in the union. Education is one of the state's largest employing industries. In the New England states outside Massachusetts, Connecticut, and Vermont, less than the national average proportion of women work in the professions.

Black and other minority professional women in New England find it more difficult than other women to obtain professional employment.[1] The limitations on the career options of black professional women with four or more years of college is especially marked in Massachusetts. There, only 67.5 percent of black women, compared to 74.4 percent of all women with the same education, are in professional posts. The highest proportion of black professional women with any college education in the state are registered nurses, about one-third of the total.

In Connecticut and Rhode Island, black professional women with four or more years of college appear to be about as likely as other women with the same education to be in the professions, over half of them as teachers in elementary and secondary schools. But at almost all other levels of education, black and Spanish-language women are less likely to hold professional jobs than other women who have the same number of years of school.

Women Professionals Are Paid Less than Men

Nationally, professional women are relatively better paid, compared to men, than are women workers in general. While the median year-round full-time earnings of women nationally are about 57 percent of men's, those of professional women are about 67 percent of men's.[2] In New England, however, as Table 9.1 indicates, professional women's wages tend to be somewhat lower as a proportion of men's than nationally. In no job category is the median income of professional women

Table 9.1

Median Earnings of Professional Women as a Percentage of Median Earnings of
Professional Men in New England, 1970

State	Annual Median Full-Time Wage of Women	Annual Median Full-Time Wage of Women as Percentage of Median Full-Time Wage of Men
Connecticut	$7,040	56.4
Maine	6,155	65.1
Massachusetts	7,196	60.7
New Hampshire	6,070	56.8
Rhode Island	6,628	62.6
Vermont	6,441	62.4

Source: U. S., Department of Commerce, Census of Population, 1970
(Washington, D.C., Government Printing Office, 1970), "Characteristics
of Population (by State)", Tables 175, 176.

reported as $15,000 or more, whereas, for several categories,
male medians are above that level. The explanation for the
relatively low wages of New England professional women
seems to lie in the particular way institutionalized attitudes
toward women in paid work interact with the regional conditions of supply and demand for these highly trained workers.

The changes in the structure of the New England
economy have led to some significant changes in the demand
for women professionals over the last decade. Their current
status is detailed in Table 9.2 for the nation and for the six
New England states.

Like other major employment categories, the professions
consist of a number of independent and differently functioning labor markets. The national market for college teachers,
for example, operates differently from the local labor market
in which social workers operate. Individuals may, over the
course of their employment history, work in a number of
labor market settings, moving across occupational categories
as well as within the overall professional grouping.

Greater numbers of men are entering many of the profes-

Table 9.2

Percent Distribution of Employed Females by Occupation, 1970, New England States and United States

	Maine	New Hampshire	Vermont	Massachusetts	Rhode Island	Connecticut	New England	United States
All employed female workers (number)	100% 140,205	100% 114,398	100% 63,174	100% 926,302	100% 151,428	100% 486,044	100% 1,881,551	100% 28,929,845
Total professional employed females	15.1*	15.3	18.1	17.3	14.1*	17.1	16.7	15.7
Nurses	3.6	3.9	4.2	3.9	2.9	3.5	3.7	2.8
Health workers, except nurses	1.0	0.9	1.2	1.3	1.1	1.2	1.2	1.1
Teachers, elementary and secondary	6.5	5.5	7.4	5.8	5.2	6.5	6.0	6.2
Technicians, except health	0.2	0.3	0.4	0.4	0.3	0.4	0.4	0.4
Other professionals	3.7	4.7	4.9	5.9	4.5	5.5	5.4	5.3
All other occupations	84.9	84.7	81.9	82.7	85.9	82.9	83.3	84.3

Source: U. S., Department of Commerce, Census of the Population, 1970 (Washington, D.C., Government Printing Office, 1970), "Characteristics of Population (by State)", Table 168.

Note: *Subcategories do not add up to this total because of rounding.

sional occupations where traditionally relatively large numbers of women have been employed. There was a marked decline in the proportion of women employed as librarians and elementary and secondary school teachers, for example, in every New England state during the 1960s. This may reflect the impact of veterans' preferences, as well as changing attitudes towards "women's work" in an increasingly crowded market. Other relatively new, rapidly growing fields, like computer work, appear to be still relatively fluid with respect to sex typing, but there seems to be a tendency for the proportion of women to decline.

Projected Trends

Estimates of expected occupational changes derived from industrial projections provide a rough indication of directions of occupational expansion in the years ahead. In Connecticut, for example, the strength of employment expansion in the professions is expected to be in engineering of all types, medical work (for example, nurses), noncollege teaching, art, and writing. Areas requiring mathematical expertise, like engineering, accounting, and computer specialties, will expand significantly in several states in the region. A breakdown of projects by sex is not available. The extent to which women participate in the expanding employment will, however, depend not only on women's training, but also on changes in the hiring and practices of the relevant employers.

Recessions increase competition for available jobs among qualified candidates. Thus, the recession in the seventies has created a greater competition between women and men and among qualified women with different kinds of training. Some occupations in which women work, like education, are more heavily affected by the recession than others. Particular attention should be paid to these occupations and the problems of women workers associated with them.

Limited Educational Options

More than in most employment categories, the supply of professional women reflects the influence of their past formal education and training experience. Almost all professionals today must have a college degree. Increasing numbers of them have also acquired postgraduate training.[3]

Most college and postgraduate education for women, nationally and in New England, has been profoundly influenced by attitudes and practices stemming from traditional perceptions as to women's appropriate societal role. A comprehensive study, *Barriers to Women's Participation in Post-Secondary Education,* prepared by the National Center of Educational Statistics, concludes:

> The variables that account for the underrepresentation of women in post-secondary education are of three fairly distinct types: (1) Policies and practices within educational institutions that actively discriminate against women or fail to encourage and support their entrance and/or continuance; (2) social constraints in the life situations of many women which mitigate against their participation in educational programs; and (3) psychological and social factors prevalent in our society that result, for some women, in negative attitudes and expectations about post-secondary education.
>
> The various factors are not independent of each other, but are interactive and as such can and do negatively influence a woman's decision to continue her education.[4]

Beliefs about women's familial role appear particularly pervasive in shaping their postsecondary school choices. If a woman does wish to enter paid work, she is expected to train for a profession that is compatible with her primary role as housewife and mother. Men's educational experiences, and hence their career options, are far broader.

There is more documentation of sex differences in participation in higher education than for other types of education beyond high school. Women are underrepresented as students in most types of postsecondary education, especially in those leading to a certificate or a degree. The exceptions are programs offering preparation for such "women's occupations" as nursing, elementary school teaching, home economics, beauty culture, clerical trades, and undergraduate programs in which women have traditionally enrolled, such as the humanities. The impact of these factors in shaping women's higher education is revealed in the available national statistics. In the United States, young women are more apt than are young men to complete secondary school; 1,286,087 males and 1,302,938 females graduated from public high schools in 1970. But fewer women than men continue their education beyond the secondary level. Among students capable of college level work, 65 percent of the men enter college and 45 percent graduate. Among women of comparable ability, only 50 percent enter and 30 percent graduate. This trend, which has persisted since the early years of this century, is projected to continue at least through 1985.

The total number of women receiving degrees at the B.A. level and beyond has almost tripled in little more than two decades from 1948 to 1970. The number holding M.A.s multiplied over six times to 83 thousand. Those with doctoral degrees multiplied eight times to four thousand. Yet women still obtained only 13.3 percent of all Ph.D.s, 39.7 percent of all M.A.s, and 41.5 percent of all B.A.s in the latter year.

Higher education for women still tends to be concentrated in a few fields. In the late 1960s, over one-third majored in education and almost half in the humanities. At the master's degree level, about half of all women's degrees were in education and nearly 85 percent were in education and the humanities. In contrast, there was a relative decline in the proportions of women taking degrees in the hard sciences, including life sciences, and most professional fields other than health and education. Even in health, there was a relative decline in the proportion of women obtaining Ph.D.s, although there was a slight increase in the proportion obtaining M.A.s. Only 8 percent of medical school students in 1970 were women. Hardly any women took doctorates in forestry, law, geophysics, metallurgy, or meteorology.

Women receive the majority of bachelor's degrees in only eight of the twenty-four disciplines. Even where women held the majority of bachelor's degrees, they received less than one-fourth of the master's and doctoral degrees in all fields except foreign languages in 1970–71. In the same year, women received only 1 percent of all first professional degrees in dentistry, 9 percent in medicine, 8 percent in veterinary medicine, and 7 percent in law.

Women tend to be overrepresented in shorter, less demanding programs and underrepresented in longer ones that lead more readily into higher-paying employment or further education. In programs of two or more but less than four years, in science- or engineering-related curricula, women earned only 38 percent of the associate degrees or other awards. They earned 47 percent of such degrees in nonscience- and nonengineering-related curricula. In programs of at least one but less than two years, in contrast, women earned 55 percent of the degrees awarded in science- and engineering-related curricula and 69 percent of those awarded in non-science- and nonengineering-related curricula.

Trends are similar in vocational and technical education in proprietary as well as publicly supported institutions. Half of the students in training programs for lower paying "growth" occupations were female, over 80 percent of them in office and health fields. Over 80 percent of the males were in computer and technical areas, where pay and status are higher. Women made up only 9 percent of the enrollment in trade and industrial programs. At any age level and at any stage of the life cycle, men are more apt than women to be enrolled in adult education courses for credit and certificates, diplomas, or degrees.

The Labor Reserve of Professional Women

The proportion of professional women who worked at some time between 1960 and 1970, but are not now earning salaries is significantly smaller than the proportion of women in the overall labor reserve of those who have worked previously (see Table 9.3).[5] This probably reflects the availability to professionally trained women of more interesting kinds of work, as well as the influence of their education on their aspirations. Their higher salaries, also, enable them to finance adequate substitutes for their own work at home, whether in the form of household appliances, household workers, or child care facilities.

The largest proportion of women in the professional labor reserve (about two-thirds), however, are trained as

Table 9.3

Females in the Labor Reserve Who Last Worked between 1960 and 1970, U.S.

	Number	Percent of Total
Total women, 16 years and older	17,461,616	100.0
Professional, technical, and kindred workers	2,003,210	11.5
All other occupations	15,458,406	88.5

Source: U. S., Department of Commerce, Census of Population, 1970 (Washington, D.C., Government Printing Office, 1970), "Subject Reports: Persons Not Employed, PC(2)-6B", Tables 12, 13.

teachers (44.8 percent) and health workers (24 percent). In both cases, there are already more women in the reserve than the projected job openings for the next few years. Many more women are currently training for these fields. If the women in the reserve seek to return to the work for which they are trained when their children are older, they will find the competition severe.

Changing Perspectives on Education

The participants in the professional workshop analyzed a number of the problems confronting women seeking advancement in professional careers. First, given the evident existing overcrowding in the educational and to a lesser extent the health fields, they emphasized the need to change the institutionalized pressures that have tended to encourage women to enter these fields. Among these are women's own, as well as those of their families, perceptions of their future career possibilities. There is some evidence that more husbands in professional families are willing to share household responsibilities than in other categories of workers, thus freeing their wives for more extensive professional responsibilities.

A shift has already begun to take place, as Table 9.4 illustrates. The probable career choices of both men and women college freshmen show a sharp decline in the per-

Table 9.4

Probable Career Choices of College Freshmen, by Sex (Weighted National Norms)
in 1966 and 1971 in Percentages

	1966		1971	
	Women	Men	Women	Men
Businessperson	3.3	18.6	4.4	16.1
Lawyer	0.7	6.7	1.4	6.8
Engineer	0.2	16.3	0.2	9.7
College teacher	1.5	2.1	0.6	0.8
Teacher, elementary and secondary	34.1	11.3	24.8	7.5
Physician or dentist	1.7	7.4	2.0	6.4
Nurse	5.3	----	8.6	----
Other health professions	6.6	3.2	8.8	4.1
Research scientist	1.9	4.9	1.5	3.3
Farmer or forester	0.2	3.2	0.7	4.8
Clergyperson	0.8	1.2	0.2	1.0
Artist (including performer)	8.9	4.6	7.2	4.9
Other choice	31.0	15.8	26.1	21.7
Undecided	3.6	5.0	13.5	12.9
[a]Total	99.8	100.3	100.0	100.0

Source: American Council on Education: National Norms for Entering
College Freshmen, Washington, D.C., annual, 1966 to 1971 (title varies
slightly). Cited in Carnegie Commission, College Graduates and Jobs:
Adjusting to New Labor Market Situation (New York, McGraw-Hill Book Company,
April 1973).

Note: [a]Totals may differ from 100.0 because of rounding.

centage opting for education. One-fourth of the women still
planned educational careers in 1971, but that figure was
more in keeping than in the past with the projected growth
of teaching posts, unless larger numbers of men opt for them
in the tightened labor market. There was a sharp increase in
the proportion of those undecided, apparently reflecting the
impact of changing career possibilities and perhaps the deep-
ening recession.

Since 1971, more women have opted for nontraditional
professions. The total enrollment of women in law schools
rose from 12 percent in 1972 to 19 percent in 1974. The
same trend may be seen in total enrollments in medical
schools, in which women represented 13 percent in 1972 and
18 percent in 1974. The increasing proportion of women in
the first year classes of these programs suggests that these

trends will continue.[6]

As women's aspirations rise, however, they still seem to think in narrow terms about professional schools, emphasizing medicine and law, while ignoring other attractive possibilities. The workshop participants pointed out that women should be encouraged to broaden their career perspectives. New professions are developing, and traditional professions like medicine and law are changing. The criteria and processes of determining credentials are being challenged. Ways need to be devised to inform women of the range of changes being made and their implications for training and work choices. Is paraprofessional work a career route into medicine or law, or is it and must it necessarily be a dead end? How can a woman become a computer programmer and rise on the career ladder in the computer field?

Workshop participants observed that women who pioneer in traditional male professions need special skills in addition to those typically taught in most professional programs. Not only must they learn to be independent, but they also need the understanding and stamina to cope with insecure and hostile male colleagues and supervisors. They need to acquire knowledge about professional styles and networks. Institutional programs need to be reappraised to ensure that they help women acquire these skills. Role models and contact with other women professionals need to be provided to ensure that they have adequate support.

Improving Placement Procedures

The second set of institutionalized obstacles considered by the workshop participants related to mechanisms for placing professional women. Many studies seek to explain how occupational segregation narrows professional women's job choices.[7] Not enough attention has been focused on the inadequacies of the links between placement offices, education and training programs, and the expansion of particular professions.

In some instances, workshop participants pointed out, state educational programs in New England have not been sufficiently geared to provide the kinds of professional skills required in the particular states. In New Hampshire, for example, 35 percent of professional and technical women are employed by government. What kinds of training do women require to enter this expanding field? Where should training programs be located, in what geographical areas, and what institutions? Where are existing programs located, and how may women obtain access to them?

On the other hand, available employment procedures and agencies are not really appropriate for placing professional women. The United States Employment Service (USES) is ineffective for professionals. In the unemployment crisis of the mid-1970s, for example, regular procedures failed to meet the needs of engineers, male or female. Special employment offices had to be established to help relocate and advise those displaced. The need to improve USES procedures for the professions is of special concern for women who are often excluded from informal networks that play an important role in the recruitment of male professionals.

For professional women re-entering the paid labor market, the issue of placement is somewhat different. Their interests may have changed; their skills may be obsolete; they may have acquired new skills in the course of their lives; or new occupations and market needs may have arisen since they completed their formal education. These women may need help in realistically assessing their talents, reviewing occupational opportunities, and making wise choices about training and career directions. At the same time, it is necessary to help them balance the need for security and transferability of skills with occupational directions influenced by their own personal interests and, in some instances, those of their families.

Special problems confront women graduates from New England institutions of higher learning who wish to remain in the region. New England is an educational center. College placement officers repeatedly note that recent graduates are interested in obtaining jobs in the region whether or not they originate there. This may be one of the factors that has contributed to a relative oversupply of professional women in the region and the relative decline of their wages below the national average in comparison to men.

Women in college and university teaching, although only a tiny proportion of all professional women, confront particular kinds of barriers to placement and upgrading. This issue is especially important in New England because of the large number of academic institutions and academically employed persons and the increasing numbers of female Ph.D.s. Women in college level teaching operate in a national market in which placement tends to take place through informal male networks. The names of qualified women need to be added to lists of applicants identified through traditional routes. Although there is evidence that young postdoctoral women have been receiving greater opportunities,[8] much more needs to be done.

Since publishing is critical to academic promotion, it may be necessary to provide special encouragement to women in their research efforts. It may be, too, that special attention should be directed to assisting women with Ph.D.s to find alternative openings as the number of academic openings are reduced due to the relative decline in the college population.

Affirmative Action?

The workshop participants explored a third set of institutionalized practices: those that thwart the advancement of women up the ladder of a professional career once they have obtained a post. Similar prejudices operate here as in other work categories to confine women to the lower paying, less prestigious posts. When promotion opportunities come along, it is most frequently the man who is offered the chance. Employers frequently perceive women, even when they are professionals, as assistants rather than directors of programs. Although affirmative action regulations have had some impact here, especially in a few much-publicized cases, it remains true that women tend to be left in the less secure, untenured, lower-paying ranks. The unemployment prevalent in New England in the mid-1970s appears to have further aggravated this problem.

Professional women are more likely to know of their rights under the legislative and affirmative action rulings than less educated women. Many are, nevertheless, hesitant to utilize individual complaint procedures because of the penalties that may be inflicted in terms of the difficulties of obtaining other jobs if they lose. Prevailing high rates of unemployment make the risks even greater. The workshop participants expressed concern that even the inadequate regulations that had been won were being weakened as budgets were cut and employment opportunities reduced in the recession.

Part-time Work

The workshop participants considered the nature of part-time work available to professional women. Almost one out of six professionals works part time. Many of these are women who seek to integrate their paid work schedules with their family obligations in compliance with societal expectations. The workshop participants observed that, as more professional men begin to share family responsibilities (and pleasures) with their wives, they, as well as women, would benefit from improved part-time work opportunities and conditions of pay.

Both government and industry are experimenting with improving the status of part-time work. These efforts need to be evaluated and publicized. At the same time, attention needs to be directed to ensuring that part-time workers receive hourly pay equivalent to that of full-time workers.

Going It Alone?

One phenomenon touched on at the professional workshop is the tendency of professional women to avoid working together to improve their job and pay status. There are many women's professional associations,[9] but most conduct activities related primarily to their professions per se. In recent years, some professional women's associations have taken initiative in supporting effective implementation of affirmative action legislation as it affects the professions. The Federation of Organizations for Professional Women has begun to play a leading role in this since it was founded. But many professional women, like their male colleagues, appear to be highly motivated individuals who have been especially socialized to believe they should be able to advance on their own merits. Not infrequently, they blame themselves, rather than institutionalized discriminatory practices, for their failure to advance in their fields.

A factor in the widespread failure of professional women to coordinate their efforts to improve their status is the tendency on the part of some to stand aloof from clerical and other women who may be employed by the same organization. Instead of seeking their friendship and involving these women in the more interesting aspects of their work, a few professional women may even try to outdo their male colleagues in their implicit (and sometimes explicit) disdain for secretarial workers in an effort to somehow prove their distinction as professionals. The most extreme case of this is the queen bee syndrome: the top professional woman who is absolutely convinced that she has achieved her status because of her exceptional qualifications and glories in her isolated position as the only woman professional. Workshop participants cited instances of such women who actually attempt to hinder the advance of other equally well-qualified women in order to retain their special status as the lone senior woman.

Competition for Grants

Competitive individualism among professional women, some workshop participants suggested, is fostered by their job insecurity. This may be aggravated by the fact that a large number of professional women must enter the annual scramble for grants merely to obtain the next year's income. This seems to be especially true in New England where an oversupply of qualified professional women makes "grants-womanship" a much sought-after career gamble.

In recent years, increasing numbers of professional women have been vying in an effort to capture a few of the dollars allocated to projects to help solve the problems of women. In the course of this project, alone, almost one hundred other Office of Education projects, throughout the nation, were identified as dealing with various aspects of women's careers. Many of them are in New England. The competitive struggle over the limited funds available—it has been estimated that less than 1 percent of all grants go to women's issues—seems to foster secretiveness and an unwillingness to join together to increase the overall impact of these kinds of projects.

Perhaps it is not too surprising, especially in periods of high unemployment, that each woman carves out her own little niche, rather than joining with others who are trying to find solutions to the same problems. The unfortunate result is that many project proposals are characterized by tunnel vision, focusing on a subjective micro-level that aids relatively few women.

The guidelines for grants sometimes function to limit their potential impact. Most proposals are treated as pilot projects, lasting only a year or so, on the apparent assumption that the project should become self-sustaining or that some other enterprise will take it over. The reality is that when a project is completed, the women whom it was designed to help, especially if they are among the most disadvantaged, seldom have the resources to continue it without outside resources; so its blueprints are simply added to the growing pile gathering dust on obscure closet shelves. The professional women who organized it, meanwhile, are compelled to bustle around to scrape up funds for a new project, entering the competitive market all over again, instead of pooling their energies in a more self-reliant endeavor.

Collective Bargaining

Professional women, as some workshop participants observed, have been even less likely than others to unite in collective bargaining actions to exert direct pressure on their employers for equity. The primary exception to this in New England has been that of the public school teachers. In recent years, as individual towns have sought to hold down property taxes by refusing to raise teachers' wages in the face of inflationary prices, increasing numbers of women, as well as men, have joined teachers' unions. In several instances, in defiance of state laws, they have conducted strikes to win higher salaries. Their new militancy and coordinated actions suggest significant changes in their objective conditions of work as well as their attitudes. This should provide a fascinating area for further policy-oriented research.

10
Managers and Administrators

The Few at the Top

It is at the top, by those who hold managerial and administrative posts, that the critical decisions are made that determine, not only who is hired and promoted, but also the overall direction of the economy in general and the professions in particular.

Here, at the top, women constitute the smallest proportion of the labor force. Women actually declined as a proportion of the management-administrative category of workers in the prosperous decade of the 1960s.

It was predicted that some 10.5 million management and administrative posts would open up nationally during the 1970s, taking into account both new and replacement positions. As more and more women with college and postgraduate degrees enter the paid labor force, it will be essential to alter the prejudices and practices operating at this level to open up more and more of these posts to them.

Traditionally, large numbers of women have not pursued careers in top management. Nor have they been actively recruited, trained, or otherwise encouraged to seek middle or senior level positions. Even institutions that have, over the years, employed high proportions of professional women workers in occupations traditionally considered female, like teaching, health care, and social work, have promoted few women to senior management positions. The same holds true for white collar firms like insurance and telephone companies and banks. Only about 5 percent of the 31.5 million women

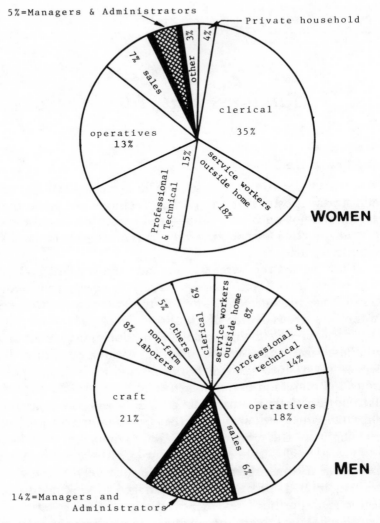

Figure 10.1 Occupational distribution of men and women in the U.S. in 1973. Source: For detailed data, see U.S., Department of Labor, Employment Standards Administration, Women's Bureau, *1975 Handbook on Workers*, Bulletin 297 (Washington, D.C., Government Printing Office, 1976), pp. 89-90.

Table 10.1

Employment Statistics for Female and Male Managers and Administrators in
New England, 1960-70

| | 1960 | | 1970 | | Percent Growth 1960-1970 | |
	Female	Male	Female	Male	Female	Male
Connecticut	10,523	75,101	14,994	92,840	42.0	24.0
Maine	4,421	24,879	5,111	25,965	1.6	4.0
Massachusetts	21,486	139,789	21,799	157,328	.01	13.0
New Hampshire	2,761	15,805	3,825	20,502	39.0	30.0
Rhode Island	2,963	21,371	3,854	21,923	30.0	2.5
Vermont	2,054	10,235	2,768	13,076	35.0	28.0

Source: U. S., Department of Commerce, Census of Population, 1970
(Washington, D.C., Government Printing Office, 1970), "Characteristics of
Population (by State)", Table 170.

in the paid labor force in 1971 were in management or administrative posts, compared to about 14 percent of all men (Fig. 10.1).

In all the New England states, with the exception of Massachusetts and Maine, the growth rate of employment of women managers and administrators exceeded that of men. In Connecticut, with the highest growth rate in New England, the employment of women at that level jumped 42 percent during the decade, compared to 24 percent for men (see Table 10.1). It should be emphasized, however, that these percentage growth rates reflect the fact that the number of women holding these positions was very small in the base year, 1960. The fact is, in spite of the higher percentage growth rates for women in these posts, that the numerical increase was less than that of men in all New England states except Rhode Island. In Connecticut, for example, the number of women managers increased by only 4,471 in contrast to an increase of 17,739 for men. In Massachusetts, where the total number of managers and administrators almost equals that of the other five New England states combined, the numbers of women employed at the top barely increased at all.

The gap between the numbers of men amd women in managerial/administrative posts actually increased in most New England states. In Massachusetts, the number of men at that level exceeded women in 1970 by 135,529 compared to 118,303 in 1960, that is by an amount almost equal to the total number of women employed in the category in 1970. In 1960, Connecticut had 64,578 more men than women in administrative positions, but by 1970 the gap had widened to 77,846. New Hampshire had only 3,044 more men than women in the top posts in 1960, but by 1970 the gap had more than quintupled.

Within the management-administration category, women are concentrated in a relatively limited number of lower level jobs, like buyers, restaurant managers, and salaried and self-employed managerial posts. The 1970 census shows that nationally only 3 percent of employed women were classified as managers. Only 420 women in that category earned over $10,000. In the Civil Service, only 16,205 women, less than 3 percent of all women in white collar government jobs, were classified in the top grades GS-12 to GS-18. They constituted only 5 percent of all federal executives, although women make up over half of all federal workers. Of the 12,000 women officers in the armed services, three-fourths were nurses.

There are few concrete facts regarding the number of women who have advanced to the top of the employment pyramid since 1970. The Census Bureau reports that the national proportion of women in management and administration rose only marginally from 15.9 percent to 18.5 percent of all those employed at that level in 1974. For those women who made it, the complex struggle for positions of equal status and acceptance has, in most instances, been a battle hard fought and far from over.

A significantly smaller proportion of black and Hispanic women hold management or administrative posts than other women with similar educational qualifications, except for those with four or more years of college. Only in Connecticut may a black woman with a college degree expect to have a slightly better opportunity than other women to obtain a management or administrative job. In Massachusetts, she may have an almost equal opportunity. There are, however, little more than one hundred black and Hispanic women with college degrees in the management and administrative category in any of the three most industrialized states in New England, compared to over three thousand in the professions. The data are, therefore, more likely to be biased by the exceptional ability of a few women or the affirmative action of a few institutions. In none of the three states are black or Hispanic women with less than four years of college as likely as other women with comparable educations to obtain management or administrative posts.

These data tend to reinforce the workshop participants' observation: A few women have been advanced in recent years to give the impression of a vigorous affirmative action compliance. In some cases, special efforts have been made to recruit highly qualified individual black women for a few select posts. But this has not changed the overall employment pattern in which discrimination thwarts upgrading of women in general and even more seriously hampers the advance of black and other minority women.

Women appointed to top management-administrative posts carry many responsibilities that are not often recognized. They must not only carry out their ordinary job responsibilities, but also must frequently convince skeptics of their willingness and ability to do so. But, as Sam Greenlee so vividly shows in his book, *The Spook Who Sat By the Door*,[1] at least some of the women who obtain high level posts are, in reality, granted visibility at seemingly new or high levels without respect or acceptance, authority or power.

The Barriers

As the participants in the management-administration workshop described the obstacles to their continued advance in terms of responsibility and pay, it became clear that many are similar to those confronted by women in the professions. The kinds of discriminatory practices that hinder the advance of women at the lower rungs of the employment ladder operate right up to the highest posts. At the top, however, they are more stringently applied, both in public and private organizations and in nonprofit as well as profit-making institutions. Women are simply overlooked in the selection of supervisory or managerial personnel.

The argument is commonly advanced that other employees, women as well as men, may object to serving under a woman administrator. But workshop participants cited several instances in which women had provided recognized competent leadership and been accepted by both. They argued that, in general, qualified women were in all respects as effective administrators as men when the organization provided the equivalent kinds of support.

The workshop participants noted, however, that a woman who is selected for the lower rungs of the management-administrative ladder is not infrequently denied the backup needed to do her job well. Many decisions in big organizations, whether public or private, are made in informal gatherings over lunch or in bars, from which women are often excluded. Top-level women must often operate alone, without the helping hand that men receive from their colleagues when they move into administration.

Administrators and managers are expected to adopt hardheaded "businesslike" attitudes, which women are more likely to have been socialized to reject. If women seek to retain a more humane outlook, their male counterparts are especially likely to be critical, refusing even to consider the possible advantages such an approach may introduce in the all-too-impersonal arena of business life.

On top of all these job-related problems, the woman manager or administrator must cope with family strains imposed by the long hours any executive must work. She has an advantage over other women working for pay in that her salary is usually high enough so she can afford to hire help or pay for other household and child care substitutes. But this does not resolve all the emotional strains that her absence from home may introduce, unless her husband is more willing than most to contribute his share to maintaining the warmth and stability required of family life.

The workshop participants emphasized that woman administrators, who leave their jobs to raise families, encounter additional problems beyond those confronting women re-entering paid jobs in other categories. (1) They have to re-establish their contacts with the management-administration personnel networks which may have been broken by their absence from the profession for a period of some years; and (2) they tend to lack confidence in their own ability to take up where they left off in competition with men who have not interrupted their careers.

Not Enough Room . . .

The participants in both the professional and the management-administration workshops underscored the fact that there are, in any event, a sharply limited number of jobs at the top. At most, perhaps one out of ten workers, male or female, can aspire to a managerial or administrative post, even if equality of access is achieved. Little more than two out of ten, at most, are likely to achieve professional status at any level. Yet today almost half of all high school students go on to college seeking to acquire the qualifications required to move into these posts. Many college graduates, especially women, are finding it increasingly difficult to find jobs commensurate with their skills.

This observation suggests the necessity of a renewed emphasis on directing managerial-administrative talents to improving the quality of worklife on all levels of the labor force pyramid. More attention needs to be focused on cooperative procedures to enable all employees, men and women, to participate in decisions shaping their conditions of work. Most women who do reach the top succeed not only through their personal efforts, but also as a result of the growing pressures for equal opportunity on a national and regional level.

The workshop members, too, noted the dangers of the queen bee syndrome and emphasized that women who do make it to the top should be encouraged to provide leader-

queen bee syndrome and emphasized that women who do make it to the top should be encouraged to provide leadership in discovering new ways to make the work experience more rewarding for both women and men employees at all levels of the workforce pyramid.

Part 4

Strategies and Action Programs To Improve the Status of Women Wage Earners

11
Toward Restructuring the World of Work

A question was posed at the beginning of this book: Why, in almost every arena of paid work, do women hold relatively unskilled jobs with ill-defined career ladders and low wages? They are seldom in the highest paid, supervisory, management, and/or administrative posts. Despite laws providing for equal opportunity and equal pay, little real change has occurred in recent decades.

The range of explanations considered by the New England workshop participants focused on the interaction of institutionalized attitudes and practices, born of a past division of labor, with the particular conditions affecting each job category in the paid labor market.

Full Employment as a Prerequisite

The difficulties of changing institutionalized attitudes and practices are, they agreed, rendered greater by the persistence of high rates of unemployment among both women and men. The fact that rates of unemployment are even higher among women than men makes it particularly difficult to initiate and implement programs to broaden their career choices.

As long as unemployment persists, employers and male employees are likely, consciously or unconsciously, to cling to the discriminatory practices and institutions that appear to function in their interests. For employers, the argument that women are only temporarily in the paid labor force provides justification for the failure to improve their pay and upgrade their skills in periods of prosperity. At the same time, it rationalizes laying women off in periods of recession. For male workers, the argument bolsters shortsighted exclusion of women from jobs and unions they perceive as "theirs," even though in the long run these practices weaken women's effective participation in the collective bargaining essential to improve the overall conditions of work for both men and women.

As the workshop deliberations revealed, the existence of widespread unemployment reduces government revenues and leads to severe cuts in the budgets of government agencies supposed to enforce laws providing fair employment practices. Many explanations have been advanced for the growing trend of structural unemployment. They range from the inadequacy of current monetary and fiscal policies to the inherent nature of the structure of the economy itself.

Some business and government spokespersons have argued that the increasing numbers of women taking paid jobs have aggravated mounting unemployment. Yet the participants in the Wellesley project underscored the fact that most women who seek paid jobs do so because of economic need. The fact that wages of large numbers of men in New England are below the minimum health and decency level appears to be an important factor contributing to the increasing numbers of women entering the paid labor force. Unemployment further reduces the levels of living enjoyed by the families of laid-off employees.

The experience of the last decade suggests that manipulation of monetary and fiscal policies, alone, is inadequate to overcome the trends of growing long term unemployment throughout the nation. Increased public expenditures, which might expand job opportunities, are widely criticized as accelerating inflationary trends. Yet the same criticism is not directed at the large military expenditures (nearly $100 billion in 1976 and slated to be higher in 1977) that have strengthened the inflationary price-fixing capacity of large firms in basic industries. Expenditures on military items, which provide relatively few jobs, have, in fact, been expanded while expenditures for social welfare items have been cut back. Housing, schools, health, and recreational facilities, which might provide far more jobs per dollar spent, are the areas most affected by government cutbacks and high interest rates, policies supposedly designed to cut inflation.

 Social scientists and policy makers have been making more proposals for plans to ensure full employment for all, both men and women, who seek paid jobs.[1] Economists in increasing numbers are suggesting that the orthodox model that assumes competition for profit will lead to the best allocation of resources is unrealistic in light of the facts of modern technology. This is true whether one is developing analysis at the level of jobs for women or at the level of the national political economy. Modern technology has imposed economies of scale facilitating, and to some extent, necessitating a level of industrial concentration that renders meaningful competition a myth. What is needed is effective overall planning along with reorganization of essential institutions to ensure that plans made are effectively implemented. Sufficient support for these arguments has been generated that legislative proposals have been advanced to provide full employment through government action.[2]

It was noted, in the course of the Wellesley project, that technology in the United States has reached levels high enough to produce all the requirements of the society during a shorter work week for individual employees.[3] It seems probable that the 8 percent rate of unemployment current in 1975 could be eliminated if the hours of work of the labor force were reduced to, say, thirty. Wages for all those at the lower end of the pay scale, including women and minorities, would need to be raised to enable them to provide adequate family support by working for the shorter period. Raising wages at the lower end of the pay scale would also reduce the income gap between the high income groups and those of the majority of workers with wages below the median, whose present weekly wages are too low to support a family of four. The resulting spread of purchasing power, furthermore, should augment effective demand and stimulate increased production and employment throughout the economy. This should enable both men and women to more fully share and enjoy the pleasures and responsibilities of family life amidst the greater cultural and recreational facilities made possible by modern technology.

Much research has been conducted as to the nature of the underlying causes of unemployment in the United States. As yet little of it has been presented in a manner that the ordinary citizen can understand in order to draw conclusions as to the appropriate strategies for overcoming them. This is an issue that women, along with other lay persons in the country, are told to leave to the experts. But the "experts" have not been able to agree on the causes, far less on the solution to this fundamental problem. Meanwhile, women and their families bear the burden of the resulting persistent unemployment. As long as high unemployment persists, the participants in all the workshops concluded, it will remain difficult to expand women's opportunities to plan more interesting, better paying careers.

For Full Creative Participation at All Levels

The project participants proposed many new approaches to provide for greater flexibility and more creative participation by both men and women in the paid labor force.

The fact is that a high percentage of jobs in the paid work world are routine and dull. Hierarchical, authoritarian work patterns limit the range of opportunities for both women and men. Fewer than one in five workers, men or women, attain skilled professional, management, or administrative posts. Cooperative decision making should replace the prevailing hierarchical job structure which tends to reduce much work, typically done by women and minority employees, to unskilled, repetitive, boring tasks. The introduction of flexitime and shared jobs might, at the same time, provide an opportunity for both men and women to adjust their hours of employment to meet family needs.[4] These measures would increase the work interest and participation of all workers.

It must be emphasized that restructuring the world of paid work to permit women to play a fuller and more equal role in the paid labor force requires, simultaneously, a restructuring of the world of work at home. The husband and children can no longer assume that the wife/mother/sister will carry on all the housework and child care, regardless of her paid work responsibilities outside the home. Instead, they too need to participate in a more cooperative sharing pattern. If both husband and wife have access to a shorter work week on the job, both will have the greater leisure necessary to enjoy the family and associated cultural and recreational activities. This would facilitate adoption of the more cooperative approach.

If restructuring the world of work on the job and at home is to become a reality, it requires a fundamental change in the entire set of attitudes and institutions governing women's participation in paid employment. The objective technological conditions are overripe for these changes.

The Need for Unity

Women who seek to improve their status and income in the paid labor force need to be in the forefront of efforts to achieve these necessary changes. Although traditionally women have organized in community groups to promote their interests in homes, churches, and schools, most do not seem to perceive the need to develop similar networks to improve their careers.

Three kinds of divisions seem to hinder women from working together to press for full employment and improvement in their conditions of work. First, a general "atomization" process seems to separate women from each other. Each tries to solve her problems alone, or as a member of a small group, instead of reaching out to cooperate with the many other women in the same situation. The workshop participants stressed the necessity of joining together in strong women's organizations to press for an end to the discriminatory practices that thwart improvement in their job status. At the same time, it is essential for women wage earners to join together with likeminded men in effective collective bargaining units.

A second kind of division that hampers women from working together is drawn along socioeconomic class lines. The blue collar, clerical, and service workshop participants pointed out that the issues they dealt with concerned about 80 percent of the women who work for pay in New England. Yet women in professions and managerial posts often fail to understand that many employed women are locked into poverty by their low-paying, dead-end jobs.

Some service workers also noted that a few women professionals, while advocating improved status for women in general, do nothing to improve the pay and benefits of women they hire to care for their children and homes. The service workers felt that the major women's organizations, led by women who have more free time because their higher incomes enable them to employ household workers or house-work-saving devices, have not adequately supported their efforts to win better wages and working conditions.

Thirdly, women's activities in New England tend to be divided along racial and ethnic lines. These divisions tend to thwart women's efforts to work together to improve their educational and employment opportunities in given localities. The workshop participants stressed that women's organizations need to involve black and other minority women at all levels, including decision making and planning, in programs to change the attitudes and institutions that impose job inequality on women. It is crucial that white women understand and participate actively in this process in order to achieve the kind of cooperation that is essential to ensure broader employment opportunities for all women.

12
Some Specific Proposals

The participants in each workshop, drawing on their specialized knowledge of the details of the New England scene, made many proposals that they anticipated could contribute significantly to overcoming the obstacles that have in the past thwarted the advance of women in the world of paid work. The three proposals that appeared most fruitful from each workshop are outlined below.[1] (In some instances, similar proposals from several workshops have been combined.)

Workshop I: Women (Re)entering the Paid Labor Force

1. *A job-focused informational-educational network.* To ensure that up-to-date information on job openings in the region is quickly available, a job-focused network should be established among educational institutions, employers, and women in cooperation with state and federal governments. The offices of the State Division of Employment Security should be required to collect statistics on current employment and unemployment by sex, as well as gather information from regional employers about their employment plans over the next decade. All this information should be disseminated through the job-focused network. Community libraries should maintain files on existing and potential career opportunities for women. Community schools and colleges could use the information to counsel women seeking to (re)enter the labor force.

The information could be used to develop educational programs to give women the skills required by the area's employers. Secondary schools, colleges, adult and continuing education programs in the region should be given the resources to bring influential regional employers and educators together to develop these programs. Programs to evaluate and assess the experience women have gained as mothers, house managers, and volunteer workers should be included.

In rural areas, an office of ombudswoman should be established to identify community resources and sympathetic persons to assist rural women seeking paid jobs. Mobile caravans could transport audiovisual materials and personnel to rural schools to enable girls in remote areas to learn of potential careers and to provide facilities for them to acquire needed skills.

2. *An unemployed women's organization.* Unemployed women should organize to press for improved information and training services for those seeking jobs. An informational handbook should be prepared to describe the kinds of service agencies available in the region for job counseling and training.

3. *Improved funding procedures.* Funding agencies could contribute to network building and ongoing cooperation by specifying, in all guidelines for granting of funds, the necessity for cooperation among women's groups across economic, racial, and ethnic lines. Other suggestions included: (1) the organization of workshops on funding, proposal writing, and sharing of data; and (2) the development of a foundation run by and for women to help women's organizations become financially self-sufficient.

Workshop II: Blacks and Other Minority Women

1. *The necessity for united action by women.* Black and other minority women should be involved in all phases of the design and inplementation of women's career projects. White women, who have greater access to sources of funds and other resources required for implementing such projects in the region, need to ensure that blacks and other minorities are included in top-level planning activities as well as in the target groups. Funding agencies should incorporate provisions to this effect in guidelines for grants and contracts.

2. *Career planning.* Special efforts need to be made to provide broader skills and career education programs for black and other minority women who do not have access to better-financed vocational and guidance programs available in suburban areas. New, less traditional approaches need to be developed to help girls from differing cultural and linguistic backgrounds prepare themselves for the broad range of occupations emerging in the changing regional labor markets. Women's organizations in communities where schools are located should be involved in developing career programs for elementary through professional schools.

3. *Utilizing religious organizations.* Religious organizations have traditionally played an important political and social, as well as spiritual, role in black and other minority communities. Resources should be made available so these organizations can develop programs to assist in broadening career perspectives of young girls. These programs should disseminate information about the kinds of careers available in the larger community, counsel girls and their families to understand the possibilities and find sources of financial assistance, and run skill-training units.

Workshop III: Blue Collar Workers

1. *Women's labor education programs.* The position of women within existing labor organizations needs to be strengthened so they can expand the areas of collective bargaining, upgrade traditional female jobs, and organize unorganized women workers. The participants recommended that a program be developed to focus on collective bargaining, grievance handling, labor history, legal rights, and leadership training. The program could be housed in an existing state university labor education center. It could be supported and implemented by a coalition of universities, community colleges, adult education programs, vocational schools, high schools, and labor unions. These institutions would incorporate the labor education program, including an active outreach effort, into their existing activities.

2. *Employer exchange.* Companies need to share information about the design and implementation of affirmative

action programs for women in blue collar jobs. Many have useful experience in providing line responsibility, role models, internal recruitment, informal training, and job exposure. Men in leadership positions in companies and unions who are knowledgeable about and committed to issues of women and work should be encouraged to work with their peers in similar policy and line positions in other organizations. A list of them should be developed and made available to the public.

Communication and coordination of this kind of exchange could be developed through such groups as the regional National Alliance of Businessmen, American Management Association, state industrial associations, business schools like Harvard and the Massachusetts Institute of Technology, and associations of affirmative action coordinators. The New England Federation of Organizations for Professional Women might take initial steps to facilitate communication and coordination.

3. *Vocational education and high school counselor programs.* The well-documented sex stereotyping in vocational education programs might be reduced by working directly with counselors. Workshop participants recommended that members of the Vocational Education Advisory Councils consider setting up intensive summer institutes for vocational education and high school counselors. The purpose would be to help them overcome sex stereotyping and to formulate programs so they could help women plan more appropriate work lives.

Since this proposal is directly related to the implementation of Title IX of the Education Amendments of 1972, as amended, initial contact should be made with the Office for Civil Rights in the Department of Health, Education, and Welfare to ascertain the type and extent of existing enforcement effort. Contact should also be made with the Project for Equal Education Rights in Washington, D.C., funded by a private foundation to monitor Title IX's implementation.

Workshop IV: Clerical Workers

1. *Redesigned vocational materials.* A packet of materials

should be prepared to help girls obtaining clerical skills in secondary and vocational schools to develop a long-term view of their careers, learn to protect their rights, and maximize their chances for meaningful work. The packet should include facts about (1) the legal rights of women as employees; (2) probable career paths open to clerical workers in large public and private organizations; (3) labor history and basic information about the role of collective bargaining for improving workers' conditions; (4) information about alternative career paths for women; and (5) techniques for learning key information about prospective employers, including their policies relating to salaries, benefits, and job promotion. The packet should be prepared by secondary school teachers of commercial courses working with resource persons and tested for use by clerical workers familiar with the problems in the field.

2. *Regional organizing seminars.* There is a need to train women who are interested in organizing clerical workers. As a previously unorganized group, clerical workers must be approached in ways that may differ from traditional union strategies. It is recommended that special programs be offered in the New England region to provide training for potential organizers. This training would be based on the special techniques developed by "9 to 5" (a Boston-based office workers' organization), District 65, AFSCME, and other unions interested and experienced in organizing clerical workers. The training would concentrate on skills in providing information on legal rights, developing networks of interested employees within an organization, researching the position of clerical workers within an organization, and handling grievances. Interested clerical workers could be recruited through postings in women's organizations (such as YWCA, women's centers, etc.) and community and state colleges.

The program could be sponsored under the aegis of the labor education program recommended by Workshop III. Other possible funding sources are adult education programs and the Women's Education Equity Act.

3. *Legislative workshops.* Legislation is needed to regulate agencies that deal with temporary clerical workers and

ensure payment of benefits. Realizing that most women workers lack information about the political steps required for passing such legislation, the participants of this workshop recommended special measures to enable women workers to establish liaison with legislators and become more effective in articulating their concerns. These include: (1) development of a handbook for each state containing basic information about each legislator, legislation that might affect the employment status of women, and a description of lobbying techniques and laws governing lobbying; (2) a reception for legislators organized by a coalition of clerical workers and other women's organizations, followed by workshops to discuss legislation affecting women in paid work.

Workshop V: Service Workers

1. *Hiring hall for service workers.* Service workers have difficulty obtaining regular employment under standardized conditions that allow them to upgrade their skills and income. Some employers have difficulty in locating qualified service workers. The service workshop participants recommended that a "hiring hall" or employment center be established in Boston to assist service workers by providing: (1) an effective way to locate job openings; (2) a skills-training program to enable service workers to improve and certify their skills and explore alternative career paths; (3) an opportunity for workers to learn their rights and collective bargaining techniques (possibly through coordination with the labor education program proposed by Workshop III); (4) a base for getting written contracts with employers to ensure regularity and improvement of employment, wages, and benefits; and (5) a center for women service workers to develop cooperative methods for providing services, laying the foundation for the introduction of better equipment, improved efficiency, and better incomes. If successful, similar centers might be established throughout the nation.

2. *Establishing credentials for service skills.* Most service jobs, especially those employing women, are characterized by ill-defined grades and low pay. Yet these jobs require increasingly complex skills, including the operation of machinery,

child care, and care of the ill and aged. The credentials of skilled workers should be recognized and rewarded by higher pay. Educational institutions should develop programs to give credentials to women who have obtained on-the-job training, especially for jobs with low-paid entry levels. These programs could be linked to high school and vocational school programs to provide for advancement up more clearly defined service-work career ladders.

3. *Workers' compensation.* Household workers have not generally had any form of insurance for job-related accidents. The workshop participants recommended that a network of women's organizations in the state be informed of the significance of legislation pending in Massachusetts on this matter and urged to express their support. The bill could provide a model for similar legislation in other states.

Workshop VI: Professional Workers

1. *"Job swapping" to improve the quality of work life.* Affirmative action may help to advance a few women into top-level management and administrative posts, but the quality of work of those who will probably remain in the same job for most of their lives must be improved. One proposal was to develop administrative arrangements to encourage workers performing similar jobs in different institutions in a given locality to "swap jobs" (that is, exchange jobs for a period of time, say a year). The job swap would offer professionals many of the same benefits as sabbatical leaves in academia: a break in customary work rhythms; a new network of work and friendship contacts; different work environments, procedural arrangements, and skills; and an awareness of alternative uses of time, interests, and preretirement directions. Employers would benefit from resulting stimulation and increased job satisfaction, as well as the introduction of new ideas and procedural suggestions. Periodic seminar meetings would permit job swappers to share and interpret their experiences. This would enhance the quality of work life and provide opportunities for lateral career movement.

The Intergovernmental Personnel Act at the national level already encourages "loans" or mobility assignments among federal, state, and local agencies and universities. An Executive Interchange Program arranges job swapping from federal agencies to private industry and vice versa. Each could provide a base of experience for implementing this proposal in New England.

2. *A managerial-administrative internship program for professional women.* The training of many women is limited to professional occupations, like teaching, where openings are scarce. A small internship program could be established to enable adult women to acquire experience to work outside their professions while acquainting employers with the potential uses of their skills. A mentor/mentee relationship within the organization would be identified for each intern. This would maximize the intern's learning about the private sector, provide her with a sense of participation in it, permit her to acquire and adapt experience with needed marketable skills, and help her to establish networks for occupational connection and advancement. A pilot project, now underway along these lines at Northeastern University in Boston, may provide useful experience for others interested in replicating it.

3. *Career planning for rural women.* Rural girls appear less aware of the need to acquire skills and plan for a meaningful career than those in urban schools. The workshop participants proposed that a project be designed to help young rural women think more realistically about their life perspectives. A pilot project, proposed for the school systems in New Hampshire and Vermont, will bring together a group of teachers of family-life programs, other professionals, and rural women to develop a trial unit to be introduced into family-life programs. The unit will be designed to help rural teenage girls understand the probability that they will of necessity have to work in paid jobs for much of their adult life and to help them to acquire the skills needed for more meaningful careers. The unit will be tested in a variety of school situations, and packaged materials will be made available for other localities.[2]

Workshop VII: Managers and Administrators

1. *Top executive seminars.* Seminars should bring senior executives from private industry for discussion with leaders

of institutions of higher education to: (1) discuss the problems and concerns for women in management and administration identified at Workshop VII, as well as others they might identify from their personal experiences; (2) formulate action programs for women at entry, middle, and senior levels; (3) evaluate past and present affirmative action efforts, their successes and limitations as they relate to recruitment, upgrading policies and procedures, training and career development of women.

The key to a successful seminar of this type would be the identification and involvement of top executives from both groups who would be willing to play a major role in inviting other participants and developing the process and content of the workshop.

2. *Communication networks through professional associations.* Professional associations, especially management and personnel associations, could make concerted efforts to establish lines of communication with top executives through newsletters and articles on: (1) nontraditional selection, training and promotion models for entry, middle, and senior level administrators, and management positions for women; and (2) affirmative action program models for recruitment, upgrading, and short- and long-term goal setting for women and minorities.

Associations should also provide information to their members on their legal rights, career development and available training, and positions available throughout the nation.

3. *Top level inservice management training.* Many professional management consultant and training groups now train entry-, junior-, and middle-level managers; some training for managers at this level is also conducted on the job. By contrast, very little planned or coordinated guidance is given to middle- and senior-level managers, especially women. Employers should be encouraged to provide training for new middle- and senior-level women managers who, in many instances, are not "sponsored" or guided by other more experienced managers. One approach would be to make specific assignments for purposes of training or guidance that would use objective systems of goal setting and appraisal of progress and development. A bonus system could be instituted to

reward the superior training of managers. In order to assist employers who are unable to provide various levels of training within the company for middle- and senior-level managers, a directory of training programs provided by various management training groups should be developed for the New England area. Programs that are especially designed for, or particularly sensitive to, problems and concerns of women managers should be highlighted.

Changing the Media's Image of Working Women

The participants in all the workshops discussed the inadequacies of the media presentation of the role of women in the paid labor market. As a result, two meetings were held at the Center for Research on Women. They were organized by an intern funded by New England Women in Communications and cosponsored by the Federation of Organizations for Professional Women. The first meeting, held in April 1976, brought together women working in various capacities in the media networks of the region to plan an all-day extended conference that took place in June 1976. Women's organizations from New England were invited to participate. A handbook was distributed describing methods by which women's organizations could influence the media to change the image they project of working women. The conference panels were led by women media specialists who helped the participants devise strategies for providing needed information and, where necessary, exerting pressures on specific radio, newspaper, and television networks throughout the region.

A Cautionary Note

Throughout their discussions, the workshop participants expressed an uneasiness. It is relatively easy, they agreed, to produce ideas for action programs in a weekend of intensive brainstorming. Far more important and probably more difficult is the formulation and implementation of strategies to ensure that the action programs are put into effect in each community. The last workshop, designed by the convener who had participated in all the preceding ones, focused on ways of formulating such critical strategies. The next chapter contains the conclusions of that workshop.

13
A Strategy for Implementation

The Model

The final workshop provided a useful model for devising strategies to implement the proposed action programs. By working through two problem areas in the educational system, the workshop participants mapped out the key steps for introducing change in any institutional system. It is essential to lay out a map of this kind before attempting to intervene in any given system. People unfortunately frequently try to effect changes without understanding the intricacies and interrelationships of the pieces of the system they are trying to change. They often blunder into needless unproductive confrontations instead of achieving consciously planned improvements. "Casing the system" in advance, determining who is doing what to whom and why, is essential to implement proposed changes in existing institutions.

It is particularly important for women to grapple with the kinds of power questions implied in this kind of mapping process. Many women, while knowing a great deal about how the world behaves, nonetheless feel that power is somehow an uncomfortable concept and seek to repress their political instincts about its uses. Yet, without tackling these kinds of issues head on, it will be impossible to effectively implement meaningful action programs to improve women's status in the world of paid work, no matter how good they may appear on paper.

At a very simple level, the strategy formulated at the education workshop may be viewed as an integrated response to the following questions.

- What *might* we do? (an analysis of the environment in which change is to be introduced)
- What *can* we do? (an analysis of our resources)
- What do we *want* to do? (an analysis of our preferences, inclinations, values, energizing issues)
- What *should* we do? (an analysis of our organizational obligations, espoused values)

On this basis, the workshop participants formulated what is here grandly termed a model, consisting of five questions. The answers to these questions in the context of any relevant system should provide the map needed to design a strategy for introducing proposed programs to improve the status of women in paid jobs.

Answers to the five questions should:

1. Identify the relevant components of the system as related to the desired end
2. Determine where it makes the most sense to intervene in the system
3. Analyze the formal and informal constraints operating in the system
4. Identify (by name) the key actors in the system who may be expected to help or to hinder
5. Understand the standard operating procedures by which the system works

In effect, the model constitutes a way of systematically structuring a problem-oriented approach. The problem to be explained, in this instance, is how the system works to produce the present (undesired) results. The answers to the five questions should provide explanations that will lay the foundation for formulating strategies to produce more desirable results.

To illustrate the model's use, the education workshop participants analyzed in depth two major areas where change is essential if education is to contribute more positively to the advance of women in paid work: the training of teachers and education administrators, and vocational/technical education.

Teachers and administrators, the workshop participants maintained, are the front line troops of the formal educational system. They decide how the curriculum should be run, what textbooks are used, and what roles boys and girls should be expected to play in the many hours of daily classroom life. They often double as vocational counselors, formally or informally advising and encouraging girls and boys to enter certain courses leading to certain careers, while discouraging them from entering others. If teachers, the majority of whom are women, could be sensitized to the impact of sex bias on young women, they could more effectively assist them to plan and acquire the needed skills to broaden their future career paths.

The current oversupply of teachers has implications for teacher training. Fewer teachers will be hired in the next ten years. Those who have jobs will be reduced in number as a function of dropping enrollments and corresponding reductions in the teaching force. Any attempt to influence the system of education through the production of new teachers is, at the current time, going to be far less effective than in periods of expanding enrollment. This suggests that the introduction of on-the-job training and summer upgrading programs will take on more significance. Regular teacher-training intitutions may play an important role in helping to set up these programs. In the longer run, regular teacher training itself will also become more important, for the school group population is projected to increase again in the 1990s.

Improved career preparation, or, more specifically, vocational/technical training, is vital because, as the preceding workshop discussions had indicated, many young girls are presently channeled into low-level careers with inadequate credentials for entering better paying, more challenging jobs. The parts of the vocational system that emphasize preparation for work in the trades and industries represent a major source of job opportunities from which most women have been traditionally excluded. To open such institutions to women would afford them a wider range of career options. Any strategies in this area, however, must confront the "closed shop" of vocational educators and a long history of excluding females, which dates back to 1908 and the original Smith-Hughes Act that created vocational education. The system is extremely entrenched. It is even difficult to collect accurate data portraying the dimensions of the problem to be addressed.

The education workshop participants pointed out that it is necessary to map the details of each of the separate systems of teacher/administrator training and vocational/technical education in New England before devising strategies to introduce new programs into either one. Each system is qualitatively different from the other, although they clearly overlap at several points. Teacher preparation in Massachusetts, for example, is located primarily in the state college system. The delivery of vocational/technical education, in contrast, is governed differently in each labor market in each state. Both systems are undoubtedly significantly different, too, from those existing in other states and other regions. It is therefore critical to map out the specific details of each system in each state and labor market.

The workshop participants identified by name the individuals working in each piece of each system who might be expected to assist in implementing programs designed to improve the pattern of socialization and career counseling of women. They also noted who might be expected to object or put obstacles in the way of such programs. The names are deleted here for obvious reasons. The workshop participants underscored the importance of that kind of specificity, however, as an essential feature of the mapping process.

The workshop participants' tentative mapping of the teacher/administrator training and vocational/technical educational systems is outlined below. As is the case with the hypotheses suggested by any model, the initial ideas they proposed must be considered tentative, subject to rigorous subsequent testing and revision. The actual testing in these instances would occur in the process of trying to implement the strategies that the mapping process suggests. Those engaged in the implementation activities must always be sensitive to changes they will need to make in their strategies and tactics as they proceed.

The Teacher/Administrator Training System in Massachusetts

1. *What are the relevant components of the system as related to the goal?*

The formal system	State colleges, private colleges, universities
The informal system	The state college system produces the vast majority of teachers; Harvard, Boston University, and Northeastern are peripheral
Relevant aspects of other formal systems that impinge	State legislature
Political groups and alignments	Key legislators and key actors in universities provide major political clout
Professional associations	Massachusetts Teachers Association holds 80 percent of bargaining power in state colleges
Ad hoc groups	Varies with issues and regions
Media	*Boston Globe,* other major daily newspapers, and television networks

2. *Where in the system does it make most sense to intervene?*

Federal, state, regional, city, town, neighborhood	At state level initially, then regionally, because three regions of Massachusetts produce different actors
Who are the proposed intervenors? What resources do they possess?	Those women currently in control, if not in power in state colleges, are currently hostile but could be potential allies for a women's effort
Which parts of the system are currently in flux?	There will be a war for control of the state college system in the next few years

3. *What are the formal and informal constraints on the system?*

Budgetary control	Board of Higher Education, secretary of education, state legislature, state college provost
Hire/fire control	At local level
Laws and legislation	State legislature key force
Climate of public opinion	Generally favorable to women; far less so within the system
Professional associations and unions	Association of State College Professors, an old, not very active group;

| | existing coalition of elementary and secondary teachers is being strengthened |
| Boards, commissions, advisory associations | Board of Higher Education soon to be disbanded; State College Board |

4. *Who are the key actors in the system?*

Who has the formal power?	The State College Board and provost; the local college presidents
Who has the informal power?	The president of the University of Massachusetts, the Senate president, the House leader
Historically, who's done what, to whom, when, and why?	(Too long a story to include here, but should be analyzed as relevant)
How can we get to the person who is, or can reach, the key actors?	In this case we could focus on women and could try to get to (1) the acting provost of the state college system, who is a woman; (2) someone at Salem State College where there is an active women's group; (3) to a woman in Senate, chairman of Ways and Means, who has a close woman friend in the State Department of Education running federal programs

5. *What are the standard operating procedures?*

How do people get, keep and advance into jobs?	Need more data
What is the reward system?	Need more data
How does the money flow?	Supposedly with the governor's approval; actually through end runs to the legislature
How does influence work?	Need more data
What is the culture of the system?	First generation college-going, anti-Ivy League, heavily Catholic

Initial Strategies for Improving Teacher Training

The mapping process helps to narrow down the range of possible strategies and tactics that may be utilized to implement proposed programs. The answers to the five questions relating to teacher/administration training immediately led the workshop participants to suggest two specific strategies.

1. Create local pressure groups to demand antisexist and antiracist courses in local schools and thereby indirectly create demands on state colleges. (Massachusetts law requires that a school committee must offer a course at the request of twenty citizens.)
2. Work on issues of teacher certification (currently in flux because of new Massachusetts teacher certification law) by
   a. utilizing the existing Interstate Compact which has thirty-eight member states, one of which is Massachusetts. Minnesota, also a member state, already has an antisex and antirace bias requirement.
   b. seeking to make certification a local matter with peer

systems banding together as in Manchester, N.H., and Washington, D.C., where a particular reading course was required by a number of schools who then got the requirement accepted by the city certification board.

There are probably many more possible strategies. Further critical analysis of the details of the system laid out above, as well as experiences in attempting to implement these strategies, would undoubtedly generate more fruitful ideas.

Vocational/Technical Education in Southeastern Massachusetts

The tentative answers of the workshop participants relating to the second key area, vocational/technical education, are outlined below.

1. *What are the relevant components of the system as related to goal?*

The formal system	City-run vocational schools, regional vocational/technical schools, the Bureau of Vocational Education; the federal vocational/technical establishment, State Board of Education
The informal system	Power resides with the Massachusetts Association of Vocational Administrators (MAVA)
Relevant aspects of other formal system that impinge	State legislature
Political groups and alignments	In the 1960s, Massachusetts moved to create a

	separate system of regional vocational schools; the movement is ongoing and makes vocational education quite separate from other educational policies
Professional associations	Massachusetts Teachers Association, American Federation of Teachers in Southeastern Massachusetts, MAVA—key group
Ad hoc groups	Some leverage possible around Boston desegregation Phase III and associated groups
Media	*Boston Globe,* other major daily newspapers, and television networks

2. *Where in the system does it make most sense to intervene?*

Federal, state, regional, city, town, neighborhood	At state level and in the regional vocational/technical schools because that subsystem differs from city-run vocational schools; and at the level of major labor markets, in this case southeastern Massachusetts
	In southeastern Massachusetts, the system of vocational education encompasses vocational/technical schools, propri-

etary institutions, community colleges, Southeastern Massachusetts University (technology part), manpower CETA programs, comprehensive high schools, industry-based training programs (Honeywell, Polaroid)

Who are the intervenors? What resources do they have?

Hard to say at this point

Which parts of the system are currently in flux?

(a) Another part of the education system, namely elementary education, is having to close schools because of declining enrollments. Those buildings could be utilized for satellite vocational skills programs which would crack the system's utilization of and reliance on high-priced buildings; (b) vocational/education emphasis on crafts is in conflict with economy's orientation toward service jobs; (c) clerical function (highest projected growth) is currently being changed by technology (neither of the last two trends is having much impact on vocational/technical schools); (d) federal government's request for a proposal to develop a model for the retraining of unemployed female teachers as vocational teachers

3. *What are the formal and informal constraints on the system?*

Budgetary control	Participating towns' school boards; the Bureau of Vocational/Technical education; Chapter 70 state reimbursements (state system for monetary support)
Hire/fire control	Local vocational school administrations and school committees
Laws and legislation	Title IX has some impact; also Massachusetts State Law (c. 622) banning discrimination by sex
Climate of public opinion	Generally hostile to women entering nontraditional trade and craft jobs
Professional associations and unions	Electrical and carpentry unions most volatile in southeastern Massachusetts at present time; printers' union strong and restrictive

4. *Who are the key actors in the system?*

| Who has the formal power? | State Board of Education, |

	state commissioner, associate commissioner for vocational/technical education, local boards, and superintendents
Who has the informal power?	Massachusetts Association of Vocational Administrators. Presently a political move to remove state board's jurisdiction over vocational/technical and create own board
Historically, who's done what, to whom, when, and why?	(Too long to be included here, but needs to be analyzed, when appropriate)
How can we get to the person who is, or can reach, the key actor?	One strategy, given absence of women in the system and traditional hostility toward women, is to try to get to the men who control the system through their daughters and wives; another is to try to get to the more sympathetic State Board of Education, but their role is currently being challenged
What will we have to pay in terms of favors traded, influence, etc.?	Hard to say at this point

5. *What are the system's standard operating procedures?*

How do people get, keep,	Teachers must get cre-

and advance into jobs?	dentials at one particular state college
What is the reward system?	Connection with unions and industry very important; helps dictate nature of shops and number of seats
How does the money flow?	Through the state department to local schools; discretionary funds made available at local superintendent initiative. Very nice system because of federal investment
How does influence work?	Need more data. Probably through the Massachusetts Association of Vocational Administrators
What is the culture of the system?	Defensive, for a long time the second class citizens of education; have finally made it big; moat and castle mentality

Initial Strategies for Improving Vocational Education

The workshop participants again tentatively identified several strategies suggested by the mapping process. They include efforts to:

1. Create pressure on State Board of Education (drawbacks already noted)
2. Create a union of women in crafts if traditional unions refuse to open up
3. Utilize federal urban renewal compliance requirements

as leverage for construction jobs

4. As indicated, utilize fact of dropping enrollments in elementary schools to circumvent the moat mentality of vocational educators to create satellite skill centers

5. Seek to redirect the flow of vocational education dollars, particularly with respect to federal vocational dollars flowing into comprehensive schools (Massachusetts commissioner has attempted to do this; success remains to be seen)

6. Seek to break the credentials stranglehold of one institution by developing a coalition of institutions to offer competition in granting credentials. Such a coalition might be built around Southeastern Massachusetts University and the newly created Lowell University with some help from Boston State College

These strategies, too, would undoubtedly be elaborated or changed by further analysis and the experiences gained in the actual process of implementation.

14
Unfinished Business

The organizers and participants in the Wellesley pilot project on expanding the career options of women repeatedly emphasized that their proposals for institutional changes in New England were not, in any sense, ends in themselves. Rather they were viewed as part of a larger ongoing process of forging national pressures to better the job opportunities and incomes of women in the world of paid work. It was anticipated that the regional contacts and networks cemented in the course of the workshops would facilitate implementation of the specific recommendations for action in the region. It was hoped, too, that women elsewhere in the nation, as well as in New England, might find useful ideas among the recommendations for developing more effective programs on their own.

But the most important contribution of the Wellesley project was viewed as the development of a participatory, problem-solving model for the systematic analysis of the causes of the many obstacles thwarting women's advance in the paid labor market. Only when women wage earners, themselves, participate in analyzing the nature of particular institutions that hinder their progress will they be able to design and build the collective strength to implement more effective action programs.

Critics sometimes object that the problem-solving methods employed in the New England pilot project become enmeshed in pettifogging incremental changes that never get at the roots of the real problems. In some cases—and some people argue that the problem of women in the paid labor force is such a one—effective solutions will require fundamental alteration of the underlying institutional structures. To use a problem-solving approach in cases like these, they claim, is like applying a band-aid to cancer. What is needed is major surgery.

This criticism ignores the fact that people learn through their experience, through the process of analyzing the causes of problems they confront and evaluating the consequences of efforts to implement the solutions their analyses suggest. In this participatory process, they have an opportunity to deepen their theoretical perceptions as to the root causes of the problems as well as to improve their practical strategies to solve them.

The crucial test of the explanations, action programs, and strategies proposed by the New England project participants will be the results of efforts to put them into effect. The funding of the project, unfortunately, only financed the gathering of information, the arrangements for the workshops, and the dissemination of the recommendations. It was assumed that specific recommendations would need to obtain financial and other kinds of support from other sources. It is to be hoped, however, that as women work together to carry out programs along the lines proposed, they will continue to critically examine the results to deepen their understanding of the underlying causes of the obstacles they encounter.

The mass of the evidence produced by the workshop participants suggests that it will be difficult to alter the institutionalized practices that tend to coerce women into low-paid jobs as long as unemployment and hierarchical employment structures dominate the world of paid work. This argues persuasively that a crucial next step is to involve women in regional and national projects to design programs for broader institutional change to ensure full employment and improve the quality of work life for all those, women as well as men, who need and want paid jobs.

Notes

Chapter 1

1. U.S. Department of Labor, Employment Standards Administration, Women's Bureau, *The Earnings Gap Between Women and Men* (Washington, D.C.: Government Printing Office, 1976), Table 1, p. 6.

2. Cited in Labor Research Association, *Economic Notes,* November 1975. For background reading, see Charles Killingsworth, *Rising Unemployment: A 'Transitional Problem,'* statement to U.S. House of Representatives, Select Committee on Labor, Detroit, March 20, 1970; and "How to Read Labor Statistics," *Dollars and Cents,* May 1976.

3. There appears to be a growing discrepancy between national estimates and the combined state estimates of total employment, reinforcing arguments for revising both sets of data. *New York Times,* November 27, 1976.

4. The project was conducted pursuant to Contract 300-75-0378; however, the opinions expressed herein do not necessarily reflect the position or policy of the U.S. Office of Education, and no official endorsement by the U.S. Office of Education should be inferred. The materials presented here represent the opinions of the authors and not necessarily those of the Center, or of the Federation of Organizations of Women or Wellesley College, the co-sponsors of the center.

5. Wingspread Report, *Women in Development* (Racine, Wisc.: Johnson Foundation, 1977).

6. Persons interested in obtaining the materials prepared by the project for replication in whole or part elsewhere may write to the Center for Research on Women at Wellesley College, Wellesley, Mass., 02181.

7. Women who work as unpaid family farm members are not included in census data on farm employment. Nevertheless, in New England there are a significant number of these in the rural states of

Vermont, New Hampshire, and Maine.

8. All data relating to labor force participation and wages is from the U.S. Department of Commerce, *Census of Population, 1970* (Washington, D.C.: Government Printing Office, 1970), "Detailed Characteristics by State," unless otherwise cited.

9. In two cases, co-conveners worked together. In most cases they had the help of student research assistants. For the sake of simplicity, however, this report will refer to the conveners in the singular.

10. Originally, this category was to include sales workers as well, but it soon became apparent that it was impossible to deal with the range of issues affecting both groups in one workshop.

Chapter 2

1. Regional studies of women's employment patterns are seriously hindered by the fact that data relating to wages and employment, by sex, are systematically collected for each state by the population census, which is taken only every ten years. As a result, the most detailed information relating to the work that women do and the wages they are paid in New England is the 1970 census, based on 1969 data. Comparison of these data with earlier censuses reveals the basic trends in the employment and incomes of women in the major occupational categories in the six New England states in the post–World War II period. All data in this chapter, unless otherwise cited, are from the U.S. Department of Commerce, *Census of Population, 1970* (and earlier decades, 1960, 1950), "Detailed Characteristics by State."

2. The national estimate is based on sample data; there will not be a precise state-by-state breakdown by sex until the 1980 census is completed.

3. The median wage is a useful concept for making overall comparisons of earnings. It is considered more useful than the arithmetic average because it is not skewed by exceptionally high or low wages. It is simply the wage that is exactly in the middle of the range of wages earned by the category of workers under consideration; half of the workers earn less, half earn more.

4. Current data relating to unemployment in each state were obtained from the State Department of Employment Security for each New England state.

5. Since the State Division of Employment Security does not gather unemployment statistics by sex, this estimate was obtained by projecting the unemployment rates for women reported in the 1970 census. The U.S. Bureau of Labor Statistics does publish current samples drawn on a national basis that show higher rates of unemploy-

ment for women than for men.

6. See President Gerald R. Ford, "Budget Message," *New York Times*, January 22, 1976.

7. New England unemployment rates were reported to have declined to levels more comparable to the national rate of 7.2 percent by October 1976, so the higher rate of unemployment may not persist. How much of this may be due to withdrawal from the labor force by discouraged workers who have given up looking for jobs is not known.

Chapter 3

1. Federal policies that seek to train and employ those who might otherwise be excluded from the labor market, including women, have also been enacted. These include the establishment of the United States Employment Service (USES), with over 2,400 local public employment offices throughout the nation (162 in New England); and the Comprehensive Employment and Training Act (CETA), passed in 1973, under the direction of the Office of Manpower Development of the Department of Labor. Information relating to these may be obtained from the respective state offices dealing with them.

2. A compilation of state legislation relating to women and employment may be found in Jessica Pearson, *A Handbook of State Laws and Policies Affecting Equal Rights for Women in Education*, Report no. 62, Equal Rights for Women in Education Project (Denver: Ford Foundation, 1975).

3. This development accompanied the passage of Title VII of the Civil Rights Act of 1964 (see p. 29).

4. Duane Lockard, *Toward Equal Opportunity: A Study of State and Local Anti-Discrimination Laws* (New York: Macmillan, 1968).

5. Massachusetts League of Women Voters, *Stage House Reporter*, August 22, 1975.

6. Pearson, *A Handbook of State Laws.*

7. Information on state laws on sex discrimination and programs sponsored for other states may be obtained from the Governor's Commission on the Status of Women located in each state capital.

8. For those who might want to relate this material to their own regions, a useful starting place is a paperback volume put out by the Government Printing Office called *U.S. Government Manual.* The manual describes all federal departments and agencies and lists the regional offices that administer several federally funded programs, including those under the direction of the Department of Health, Education, and Welfare and the Department of Labor. The government manual is available in most public and college libraries.

9. The location of the offices responsible for administering these laws in each region may be obtained from the current *U.S. Government Manual* (Washington, D.C.: Government Printing Office) or from the Governor's Commission on the Status of Women for the relevant states.

10. The United States Commission on Civil Rights, established by Congress in 1957 to watchdog federal policies on discrimination because of race, color, religion, or national origin (sex discrimination was added in 1972) frequently provides detailed critiques of those policies. Since 1970 the commission has published yearly appraisals of equal opportunity legislation and implementation. Its reports are succinct and factual and traditionally include suggestions for improving national policy. They are available in libraries (listed under United States Commission on Civil Rights) and from the commission itself (1121 Vermont Avenue, NW, Washington, D.C.).

11. U.S. Commission on Civil Rights, *The Federal Civil Rights Enforcement Effort—1974,* Vol. V, "To Eliminate Employment Discrimination" (Washington, D.C.: Government Printing Office, 1975).

12. Ibid., p. 436.

13. Ibid., p. 646.

14. *New York Times,* July 8, 1977.

15. 1029 Vermont Ave., NW, Suite 800, Washington, D.C., 20005.

16. Complaints may be filed by writing to the Office for Civil Rights at the U.S. Department of Health, Education, and Welfare, 330 Independence Ave., SW, Washington, D.C., 20201, or to the nearest regional HEW civil rights office.

17. U.S. Commission on Civil Rights, *The Federal Civil Rights Enforcement—1974,* p. 289.

18. *New York Times,* June 20, 1975.

19. For a summary of grants awarded by the Office of the Assistant Secretary of Education, the Office of Education, and the National Institute of Education, see *Focus on Women, A Guide to Programs and Research in the Education Division.* The National Institute of Mental Health under HEW also has funded projects related to women's issues. Write separately to the National Science Foundation, 1800 G Street, NW, Washington, D.C., 20006; National Institute of Mental Health, 9000 Rockville Pike, Bethesda, Maryland, 20034.

Chapter 4

1. U.S. Department of Labor, Bureau of Labor Statistics, *U.S. Working Women: A Chartbook* (Washington, D.C.: Government Printing Office, 1975), Chart 25.

2. Howard Hayghe, "Marital and Family Characteristics of the

Labor Force, March 1975," *Monthly Labor Review* 98, 11 (November 1975): 55.

3. Heather L. Ross and Isabel V. Sawhill, *Time of Transition: The Growth of Families Headed by Women* (Washington, D.C.: The Urban Institute, 1975), Chapter 1.

4. Ibid.

5. U.S. Department of Labor, *U.S. Working Women: A Chartbook,* Chart 25.

6. Hayghe, "Marital and Family Characteristics," p. 55.

7. U.S. Department of Labor, *Manpower Report of the President* (Washington, D.C.: Government Printing Office, April 1975), p. 70.

8. Ibid.

9. See, for example, U.S. Office of Education, National Center of Educational Statistics, *Barriers to Women's Participation in Post-Secondary Education* (Washington, D.C.: Government Printing Office, 1975).

10. See, for example, Caroline Isber and Muriel Cantor, *Report of the Task Force on Women in Public Broadcasting* (Corporation for Public Broadcasting, 111 16th St., NW, Washington, D.C., 20036).

11. Arleen Leibowitz, "Education and Home Production," *American Economic Review* LXIV (May 1974): 243-250.

12. Ann Connolly, "Production/Consumption: An Analysis of the Relationship between Married Women's Employment Status and the Demand Patterns of Their Families" (Honors thesis, Wellesley College, 1975).

13. This is illustrated by the tiny percentage of women employed as managers and administrators, most of whom work in eating and drinking places and clothing and apparel stores. See U.S. Department of Labor, Women's Bureau, *Handbook on Women Workers, 1975,* Bulletin 297 (Washington, D.C.: Government Printing Office, 1975), p. 96.

14. U.S. Bureau of Census, *The Statistical Abstract of the United States* (Washington, D.C.: Government Printing Office, 1973), p. 238.

15. For a discussion of union attitudes toward women by industry, see Elizabeth F. Baker, *Technology and Women's Work* (New York: Columbia University Press, 1964); see also Lucretia Dewey, "Women in Labor Unions," *Monthly Labor Review* 94, no. 2 (February 1971): 42-48.

16. See A. McEwan, "Capitalist Expansion, Ideology, and Intervention," in D. C. Edwards, M. Reich, and T. E. Weisskopf, *The Capitalist System* (Englewood Cliffs, N.J.: Prentice-Hall, 1972).

17. For data on South African wages, see Cape Town SRC, Wages

Commission, "Poverty, Our Concern, Our Responsibility," in *UN Unit on Apartheid, Notes and Documents*, No. 25/74; S. Bisheuvel, "Black Industrial Labor in South Africa," in South African Congress of Trade Unions, Memorandum submitted by the South African Congress of Trade Unions to the Sixtieth Session of the International Labor Organization held in Geneva, June 1975 (London, 1975).

18. For status of women in unions in the United States, see Gladys Dickason, "Women in Labor Unions," *The Annals of the American Academy of Political and Social Sciences 251* (May 1974); Virginia Bergquist, "Women's Participation in Labor Organizations," *Monthly Labor Review* 97 (October 1974); Barbara Wertheimer and Anne Nelson, *Trade Union Women: A Study of Their Participation in New York City Locals* (New York: Praeger Publishers, 1975); and Judith Buber Agassi, "Women Who Work in Factories" in *The World of Blue Collar Workers*, Irving Howe, ed. (New York: Quadrangle Books, 1972).

19. Cf. C. W. Mills, *The New Men of Power: America's Labor Leaders* (New York: Agustus M. Kelley, 1971).

Chapter 5

1. The use of the term minorities reflects the influence of historically evolved prejudice on concepts used to discuss differing population characteristics. All groups in the United States are of different national or geographic origin. Yet the United States census lumps Polish-, Italian-, Franco-, Anglo-, Jewish-, and Irish-Americans into one category: "white," along with those Mexicans, Puerto Ricans and others who descend from "Indo-European stock." The census groups people of color together as "nonwhite" or "other races," noting, "The concept of race does not denote any scientific definition of biological stock. Rather it reflects self-identification by respondents." The census also classes persons of "mixed" parents by the "race" of the father. The term *Negro* includes all who characterized themselves as "Negro, Black, Jamaican, Trinidadian, West Indian, Haitian, or Ethiopian," and "Indian" all who call themselves Indian, Native American, or members of a tribe. Chinese, Japanese, Filipinos, and sometimes other Spanish-speaking peoples are included among "other races."

In recent years, since the term race has been rejected as unscientific, it has become common to speak of minorities. Yet this term too lacks any scientific foundation. It reflects the fact that, while distinct geographical and cultural differences of the tribes of Europe have not prevented them, over time, from being assimilated into the "majority white" population, the persistence of racism has made color the basis of a special category of minorities: Americans who cannot assimilate simply by learning the language, going to school, keeping clean, obeying the laws, and otherwise conforming to the model of a good citizen. Despite its self-evident drawbacks, the term minority is used here, for lack of a better, to focus on the special problems these women face in the world of paid employment.

2. Third World Women's Alliance, *Triple Jeopardy* (New York: 1975).

3. "Classism" refers to the assumption, commonly held in the dominant culture, that all minority persons, regardless of their achievements or actual status, are lower class.

4. Unless otherwise cited, the data in this chapter relating to the employment and incomes of black and other minority women is from the U.S. Department of Commerce, *Census of Population, 1970* (Washington, D.C.: Government Printing Office, 1970), "Characteristics by State."

5. Massachusetts State Advisory Committee Report to the U.S. Civil Rights Commission, Discrimination in Housing in the Boston Metropolitan Area (Boston: Massachusetts State Advisory Committee, 1963), pp. 20-30; see also Massachusetts State Advisory Committee Report, *Housing Discrimination in Springfield-Holyoke-Chicopee Metropolitan Area* (Boston: Massachusetts State Advisory Committee, 1966), pp. 31-40.

6. Ibid., p. 7.

7. The relatively low rate of participation by black men in the labor force, a rate that has been declining since World War II, probably reflects the greater job discouragement they experience, leading many to simply give up actively seeking employment. Maine is the only New England state where black men are reported to have a higher labor force participation than all men. It would be interesting to study the possible reasons for this, although the numbers of men appear too small for generalizations. The large apparent differences in the participation rates of all men in all three industrialized states (80.3 percent in Connecticut, 60.3 percent in Massachusetts, and 57 percent in Rhode Island) suggests, however, the need for a close examination of the data and the data-collection methods.

8. James E. Blackwell, *The Black Community, Diversity and Unity* (New York: Dodd, Mead & Co., 1975), p. 42.

9. Ibid., p. 43.

10. Many studies have been made of the special problems confronting black families and the role of women in them. A summary of arguments over the significance of these findings is to be found in Blackwell, *The Black Community*.

11. Unless otherwise cited, the information relating to Boston's Hispanic population was provided by Dr. Freda Garcia of the Massachusetts Department of Mental Health.

12. Miranda Lourdes King, "Puertoriquenas in the United States—The Impact of Double Discrimination," *Civil Rights Digest* 6, no. 3 (Washington, D.C.: U.S. Commission on Civil Rights, Spring 1974): 23.

13. "How Many Indians Were There When the White Men Came, and How Many Remain?" in Virgil J. Vogel, *This Country Was Ours* (New York: Harper & Row, 1972), pp. 250-254.

14. Ethel Boissevain, "Narragansett Survival: A Study of Group Persistence Through Adopted Traits," in D. E. Walker, *The Emergent Native American* (Boston: Little, Brown, 1972), p. 659.

15. Harold Cruse, *The Crisis of the Negro Intellectual* (New York: William Morrow and Co., 1967), pp. 64-95.

16. Robert Terry, "The White Male Club Biology and Power," *Civil Rights Digest* 6, no. 4:66-75.

17. Ibid., p. 74.

18. Massachusetts Advisory Report, *Discrimination in Housing*, p. 12.

19. Ninety-six school districts in the suburbs of the Greater Boston Metropolitan Area had a higher computative equalized property value per student attending school than did the Boston School District in the inner city. The latter obtained more federal and state funds per pupil, but its greater administrative expenditures reduced actual spending per pupil below that of many of the suburban schools. (Metropolitan Planning Project, *Metro Ways to Understanding* [Boston: MASBO Cooperative Corporation, 1974], vol. II, pt. II, Tables 24, 25.)

20. Massachusetts was the first state in the nation, in 1965, to pass a racial imbalance law. Connecticut followed, and several cities in that state made substantial progress toward implementation. The Boston school system, however, despite the new law, tended to become more segregated as its minority population grew. A new program was initiated by the Metropolitan Council for Educational Opportunities, METCO, in the early 1970s. By 1976, it was busing about 3,000 students to over 30 predominantly suburban communities. Nevertheless, segregated schooling persisted as a predominant feature of the Boston school system until the United States District Court ordered desegregation by extensive busing in 1974. Even after the court order, vociferous complaints of white antibusing forces fostered violence that disrupted schooling. Pro-integration forces worked to provide better schools in the inner cities where court-ordered busing has been in effect, but their efforts have been undermined to some extent by budget cuts designed

to hold down local property taxes. It should be noted that there has not as yet been a full evaluation of the consequences of the busing program.

Chapter 6

1. This clerical workship was originally planned to include clerical and sales workers. The conveners decided, however, that the particular problems of sales workers were sufficiently unique that they should not be combined with clerical workers. In another series of workshops relating to women's paid jobs, an entire workshop might well be devoted to the special problems of women sales workers.

2. Unless otherwise stated, the data in this chapter on employment and earnings of clerical workers are from U.S. Department of Commerce, *Census of Population, 1970,* "General Social and Economic Characteristics (by State)" (Washington, D.C.: Government Printing Office, 1970).

3. U.S. Department of Labor, Bureau of Labor Statistics, *Area Wage Survey, Boston, Massachusetts, Metropolitan Area, August 1974,* Supplement 2 to BLS Bulletin 1775-13 (Washington, D.C.: Government Printing Office, January 1975).

4. U.S. Department of Labor, Bureau of Labor Statistics, *Employment and Earnings* (Washington, D.C.: Government Printing Office), vol. 17 (October 1970); vol. 22 (October 1975).

5. Harry Braverman, *Labor and Monopoly Capital* (New York, London: Monthly Review Press, 1974), pp. 339-347, 381, 384.

6. Barbara Garson, *All the Livelong Day* (New York: Doubleday, 1975), pt. 3.

7. Evelyn Glenn amd Roslyn Feldberg, "Degraded and Deskilled: The Proletarianization of Clerical Work," *Social Problems,* October 1977.

8. Mary Kathleen Benet, *The Secretarial Ghetto* (New York: McGraw-Hill, 1972).

Chapter 7

1. See H. A. Miller, "Changes in the Number of Poor," in M. S. Gordon, *Poverty in America* (San Francisco: Chandler Publishing Co., 1965), p. 87.

2. U.S. Department of Labor, *Manpower Report of the President, 1970* (Washington, D.C.: Government Printing Office, 1970), especially pp. 92-112.

Chapter 8

1. In other regions, a larger proportion may help to earn family

income as unpaid farm workers.

2. Report of special task force to secretary of Health, Education, and Welfare Department, *Work in America* (Cambridge: Massachusetts Institute of Technology Press, 1975), pp. 29-38.

3. R. W. Ackerman, "How Companies Respond to Social Demands," *Harvard Business Review,* July-August 1973, p. 88.

4. William H. Chase, *The American Woman, Her Changing Social, Economic and Political Roles, 1920-1970* (New York: Oxford University Press, 1972), p. 76.

5. Barbara Wertheimer and Anne Nelson, *Trade Union Women: A Study of Their Participation in New York City Locals* (New York: Praeger Publishers, 1975).

6. U.S. Department of Labor, *Women in Apprenticeship—Why Not?* Manpower Research Monograph no. 35 (Washingon, D.C.: Government Printing Office, 1974).

7. Jon J. Durkin, *The Potential of Women,* Research Bulletin 87 (Washington, D.C.: Johnson O'Connor Research Foundation, 1972).

8. Jack Conrad Willars, "The Impact of Women's Liberation on Sexist Education and Its Implications for Vocational-Technical and Career Education," paper delivered to regional seminar/workshop on Women in the World of Work, Technical Education Research Centers, Department of History and Philosophy of Education, George Peabody College for Teachers, Nashville, Tennessee, 1974, p. 7.

Chapter 9

1. This is clearly shown by the census data for the states, which give occupation by sex, race, and level of education. U.S. Department of Commerce, *Census of Population, 1970* (Washington, D.C.: Government Printing Office, 1970), "Characteristics by State," Table 179.

2. U.S. Department of Commerce, Bureau of the Census, *Current Population Reports,* "Consumer Income," Series P-60, No. 93: 90.

3. We will not address the questions of whether the value of a college degree in terms of future income rewards is declining and what this means for the future of higher education for women (*New York Times,* August 14, 1975). Nor will we discuss the relative merit of a liberal arts education v. vocational training. Both, however, are relevant to career directions of educated women.

4. U.S. Office of Education, National Center of Educational Statistics, *Barriers to Women's Participation in Post-Secondary Education* (Washington, D.C.: Government Printing Office, 1975). This is the source of data relating to education of professional women unless

otherwise cited.

5. U.S. Department of Commerce, *Census of Population*, "Persons Not Employed," PC (2)-6B, pp. viii, 125. For a discussion of the concept relating to economically active populations, see Carolyn Shaw Bell, "Definitions and Data for Economic Analysis," in Ruth B. Kundsin, *Women and Success: The Anatomy of Achievement* (New York: William Morrow and Company, 1974).

6. John B. Parrish, "Women in Professional Training," *Monthly Labor Review* 97, no. 5 (May 1974): 40-43. Projections to 1985 have been made which indicate that by that date women will account for 30 percent of total enrollment in medical schools.

7. See Francine D. Blau and Carol L. Jusenius, "Economists' Approaches to Sex Segregation in the Labor Market," in Martha Blaxall and Barbara Reagan, eds., *Women in the Workplace* (Chicago: University of Chicago Press, 1976), pp. 181-199; and Hilda Kahne, "Economic Perspectives of the Roles of Women in the American Economy," *Journal of Economic Literature*, December 1975.

8. Allan Cartter and Wayne E. Ruther, "The Disappearance of Sex Discrimination in First Job Placement of New Ph.D.s," Research Report 75-1 (Los Angeles: Higher Education Research Institute, 1975).

9. Over one hundred have become affiliated with the Federation of Organizations for Professional Women, which co-sponsors the Center for Research on Women at Wellesley.

Chapter 10

1. Sam Greenlee, *The Spook Who Sat By The Door* (New York: R. W. Baran, 1969).

Chapter 11

1. Robert H. Heilbroner, "The American Plan," *New York Times Magazine*, January 25, 1976, argues: "National economic planning will arrive when businessmen demand it—and demand it they will, to save the capitalist system."

2. U.S., Congress, House, Committee on Education and Labor, *Equal Opportunity and Full Employment Act*, H.R. 50, 1609, 140, 2209 (Washington, D.C.: Government Printing Office, 1975).

3. It is often argued that managerial and professional workers have not even been able to reduce their hours to the legally required forty a week. The fact is, however, that these salaried workers are well-recompensed for their extra hours, and, at least in the case of professional people, often work longer because they enjoy what they are doing. There need be no requirement that salaried workers reduce their hours

to the legal maximum of thirty if it should be established.

4. Research might be conducted to determine whether managerial and supervisory hours of work, too, might not be reduced in the long run by the adoption of such cooperative approaches to work.

Chapter 12

1. Readers may obtain a full set of the recommendations of each workshop by writing to the Center for Research on Women, Wellesley College, Cheever House, 828 Washington Street, Wellesley, Massachusetts, 02181.

2. A participant from the professional workshop has already obtained funding for this proposal and is now implementing it. For further information, contact Faith Dunne, Education Department, Dartmouth College, Hanover, New Hampshire, 03755.

Annotated Bibliography

I. General

A. Sources of Statistical Data for the Nation and Each State

Bureau of Labor Statistics, U.S. Department of Labor, *Handbook of Statistics* (Washington, D.C., Government Printing Office, annual). This reference book compiles summary data relating to all aspects of the national labor force which is gathered for the Bureau of Labor Statistics. The BLS also publishes monthly reports on wages and employment and the *Monthly Labor Review*, which contains useful analyses of various aspects of the employment of women.

Division of Employment Security in each state, affiliated with the U.S. Department of Labor's Manpower Administration, prepares an annual manpower report. This describes the current pattern of employment and outlook by industry and occupation and discusses current unemployment trends. The current status of women and minorities is usually indicated. The division reports the occupational breakdown of the labor force by sex and minority for each major Standard Metropolitan Statistical Area (SMSA). The division has prepared employment projections for 1980 for most of the states by industry and by occupation, but not by sex or minority group. These projections are likely to differ significantly from the actual situation in 1980 since the latter will be affected by various unforeseen factors, including the current depression. The division gathers data related to current unemployment in each state, but typically it is not broken down by sex, minority, or occupation.

Ferriss, Abbott L., *Indicators of Trends in the Status of American Women* (New York, N.Y., Russell Sage Foundation, 1971). This book contains valuable charts showing the changes in female population, the trends in the educational status of women, their marital status and fertility trends, the migration of women, and the characteristics of women who work and the kinds of jobs they hold throughout the nation.

U.S., Department of Commerce, *Census of Population, 1970*, "Characteristics of Population (by state)" (Washington, D.C., Government Printing Office, 1970). The United States census, collected every ten years, is the most accurate available source of detailed characteristics of the population of each state in separate volumes. The 1970 report includes 1960 data for purposes of comparison.

U.S., Department of Commerce, Social and Economic Statistics Administration, *Social Indicators, 1973, Selected Statistics on Social Conditions and Trends in the United States* (Washington, D.C., Government Printing Office, 1973). Tables of detailed national data on employment, income, and education, by sex and race, illustrated by charts.

U.S., Department of Commerce, *U.S. Statistical Abstract* (Washington, D.C., Government Printing Office, annual). A compilation of summary data relating to all aspects of the economy collected by government agencies.

U.S., Department of Labor, Women's Bureau, has published reports for each state on *Women Workers.* These give data on the increase of women in the labor force, their ages, education, marital status, size of families, occupations, and family incomes. A special section is devoted to data on the status of black and minority women workers.

The Women's Bureau also publishes an extensive list of materials relating to various aspects of women and employment. The bureau's publication list, published periodically, reports the materials relating to these and gives their prices. Their publications include facts about women workers, why they work, who they are, turnover, and what their rights are; career opportunities for women; education and training programs; child care services; black and minority women; standards and legislation affecting women; reports of various commissions on the status of women; and conference reports. The list may be obtained from the regional office of the Women's Bureau, located in the regional U.S. Labor Department office, or from the national Women's Bureau, Employment Standards Administration, U.S. Department of Labor, Washington, D.C., 20210.

B. Selected Background Materials

Baker, Elizabeth Faulkner, *Technology and Woman's Work* (New York, Columbia University Press, 1964). Analyzes the impact of technological change in the last century and a half on women's work and the particular industries and occupations in which women have been employed. Discusses the range of factors influencing hiring and upgrading women in the categories.

Bell, Carolyn Shaw, "Age, Marriage and Jobs," *The Public Interest* no. 30 (Winter 1973): 76-87. Analyzes the causes and effects of the changing pattern of employment and the increasing numbers of women workers.

Blaxall, Martha, and Barbara Reagan, eds., *Women in the Workplace: The Implications* (Chicago, University of Chicago Press, 1976).

Keyserling, Leon H., *Full Employment Without Inflation,* prepared for the Task Force of the Committee on Full Employment, Conference on Economic Progress, 2610 Upton Street, Washington, D.C., 20008, 1975. An analysis of the economic obstacles to full employment and suggestions for a program to overcome them without too great a degree of inflation, prepared by a Task Force of the Committee on Full Employment, formed in 1974 and co-chaired by Murray H. Finlay, president, Amalgamated Clothing Workers of America (one of the unions with a high proportion of women workers) and Coretta Scott King, president, Martin Luther King Center for Social Change.

Kreps, Juanita, *Sex in the Marketplace: American Women at Work* (Baltimore, Johns Hopkins Press, 1971). Presents valuable data relating to women's status in labor force and the factors governing the supply and demand for women wage workers. Discusses the value of women's nonmarket work and the lifetime perspectives of women. Examines legislation related to women's wage employment.

——, *Women and the American Economy* (New Jersey, Prentice Hall, 1976). A collection of articles on family and work, EEO laws, and so on.

Lloyd, Cynthia B., ed., *Sex, Discrimination and the Division of Labor* (New York, Columbia University Press, 1975). Excellent assemblage of economists who write on a range of topics concerning women in the economy. Useful background for all occupational categories.

Lyle, Jerolyn R., and Jane L. Ross, *Women in Industry* (Lexington, Ky., D.C. Heath and Co., 1973). Presents statistics resulting from a study of 246 large corporations in an effort to explain the variations among the patterns in which they hire women, and attempts to relate these to theories of discrimination.

Mattila, J. Peter, *Labor Turnover and Sex Discrimination* (Iowa State University of Science and Technology, Industrial Relations Center). It has been alleged that high female labor turnover imposes costs upon employers which induce them to discriminate against women in hiring and pay. This study examines male and female quit rates and draws two primary conclusions. First, women are less likely than men to quit for job-related reasons, although they do quit more often because of household responsibilities. It is not true that total female quit rates exceed male rates. Second, female quit rates are lower relative to male rates during periods of low unemployment, which suggests the importance of maintaining full employment to combat discrimination.

Miller, Jean Baker, *Towards a New Psychology of Women* (Boston, Beacon Press, 1976) relates to power relations between subordinate and dominant groups (guess who is which) and to employment because power relations in the family and the meaning of work in those relationships is critical to women moving out.

O'Toole, James, ed., *Work and the Quality of Life, Resource Papers for Work in America* (Cambridge, Massachusetts Institute of Technology Press, 1974). This book is a compilation of papers prepared by an independent task force in 1972 for the secretary of Health, Education, and Welfare, which concludes that the institution of work provides the critical leverage for improving the quality of life in the United States. It analyzes the impact of low wages and lack of job satisfaction on the lives of workers. It includes a paper by Isabel V. Sawhill that focuses on the particular implications of the study for women; but the other papers, examining the impact of work on physical and mental health, also have significant implications for women workers. A section on education summarizes studies showing that vocational education has not significantly improved the job opportunities of those acquiring it and criticizes education in general for its inadequate contribution to improving work and the quality of life in the nation. Several chapters are devoted to examination of specific projects to redesign jobs and federal work strategies.

Sweet, James A., *Women in the Labor Force* (New York, Seminar Press, 1973). In the tradition of cross-sectional demographic studies, relates data on family status to the role of women in labor force. Looks at family status, education, economic need, and labor force activity of women. Examines black-white differences in wives' earnings and contributions to family income.

Tsuchigane, Robert, and Norton Dodge, *Economic Discrimination Against Women in the United States, Measures and Changes* (Lexington, Ky., Lexington Books, D. C. Heath and Co., 1974). Separates established indexes of income, occupational, and participation discrimination and analyzes factors affecting each of these.

U.S., Department of Labor, Women's Bureau, *Automation and Women Workers* (Washington, D.C., Government Printing Office, 1970), 12 pp. This report discusses technological developments in the United States between 1958 and 1968 that have caused changes in employment opportunities for women. The implications of these technological changes are discussed with regard to employment and unemployment, vocational guidance and training, training and retraining of older women, remuneration, hours of work and leisure, safety and health, and child care.

——, "Facts About Women's Absenteeism and Labor Turnover" (Washington, D.C., Government Printing Office, August 1969). Briefly and clearly presents information disproving traditional myths and stereotypes about women and work.

Weber, Gustavas A., "The Women's Bureau" (New York, Ams Press, 1974). Contains history of bureau, explanation of activities (research, investigations, and recommendations for women in industry, work with other agencies), and breakdown of organization into divisions of investigation, research, statistics, reports, and exhibits. Also included are financial statement, laws, publications, bibliography. Short and official.

C. *Public Policy and Sex Discrimination Legislation*

(Note: Explanations of legislation and critiques of its administration have been the substance of many articles, handbooks, and "almanacs." Reviews that explore the details of how legislation has been carried out are much more scarce. It is the latter kind of data, much of it undeveloped, with which critics of public policy should be concerned.)

Murphy, Irene L., *Public Policy on the Status of Women, Agenda and Strategy for the 70s* (Lexington, Ky., Lexington Books, 1973). A review of policy on federal level as it relates to status of women with emphasis on employment, how policy has been formed, and what its future might be.

——, *National Policy Guide for the Working Woman* (Federation of Organizations for Professional Women, 2000 P St., NW, Suite 403, Washington, D.C., 20036, 1975). Brief review of significant public policy decisions—legislative, adminstrative, and judicial—made about the status of women in 1974.

PEER *Perspective*, a newsletter that monitors the progress of Title IX, Education Amendments of 1972, and is available from 1522 Connecticut Avenue, NW, Washington, D.C., 20036.

Ross, Susan C., *The Rights of Women: The Basic ACLU Guide to a Woman's Rights* (New York, Avon Books, 1973). An excellent compilation of state and national legislation, simply written and well organized.

Sandler, Bernice, "Sex Discrimination, Educational Institutions, and the Law: A New Issue on Campus," *Journal of Law and Education,* vol. 2, no. 4 (October 1973), available from Association of American Colleges Project on the Status of Women, 1818 R St., NW, Washington, D.C., 20009. This brief article has a very helpful summary of the requirements of an affirmative action plan.

U.S., Citizens' Advisory Council on the Status of Women, *Women in 1974* (Washington, D.C., Government Printing Office, 1975). A yearly review of the activities of women as they apply to government policies, legislation passed by Congress on various aspects of feminism, and the government policies.

U.S., Commission on Civil Rights has a number of reports on the effectiveness of federal legislative efforts to bring equality in employment status to women: *Civil Rights Digest,* Sexism and Racism, Spring 1974. *Guide to Federal Laws Prohibiting Sex Discrimination. Women and Poverty,* prepared for hearing in Chicago, 1974. *Federal Civil Rights Enforcement Effort Report, 1974.*

U.S., Department of Labor, Employment Standards Administration, Wage and Hour Division, *Equal Pay for Equal Work Under the Fair Labor Standards Act* (Washington, D.C., Government Printing Office, 1972). This "interpretative bulletin" does not include the amendment made in 1972 when the act's coverage was extended to executive, administrative, and professional employees.

U.S., Department of Labor, Office of Federal Contract Compliance, Chapter 60-OFCC, *Equal Employment Opportunity Part 60-2 Affirmative Action Programs,* a reprint from Federal Register, vol. 36, no. 234, Saturday, December 4, 1971, includes changes in so-called Revised Order No. 4, on July 12, 1974.

D. *Women and Labor Unions*

Caplow, T., *The Sociology of Work* (New York, McGraw Hill, 1964). Analyzes the low pay and low levels of union organization in women's occupations.

Dewey, L. M., "Women in Labor Unions," *Monthly Labor Review* 94(2) (February 1971): 42-48. A discussion of recent activities of American women as trade union members and officers, factors influencing female union participation, and specific issues of concern for bargaining.

Faler, P., T. Dublin, and J. O'Brien, "The New England Working Class, A Bibliographic History," (Boston, Radical Historians Caucus, November 1972).

Henry, Alice, "The Trade Union Woman" (New York, Lenox Hill Publishing Company, 1973).

Myers, M. Scott, "Overcoming Union Opposition to Job Enrichment," *Harvard Business Review,* May-June 1971.

Scheible, Paul A., "Changes in Employee Compensation, 1966 to 1972," *Monthly Labor Review* 98(3) (March 1975): 10-16. Rates of increase were higher for employees in unionized establishments and for nonmanufacturing workers.

Schreiner, Olive, "Woman and Labor" (New York, Johnson Reprint, 1972). Sociological, historical approach to study of women and labor which leads up to a study of economic and social problems a woman faces in her day: lack of recognition for work done in the home, treatment as economic parasite in marriage, unequal pay for equal work and related problems. Early feminist work, which stresses value of movement and political effort on the part of women.

Wertheimer, Barbara, and Anne Nelson, *Trade Union Women: A Study of Their Participation in New York City Locals* (New York, Praeger Publishers, 1975). The only current book on women and trade unions based on New York City locals; describes women presently active in unions. Identifies barriers to women's membership and leadership with a resulting focus on education and training. Calls for action by male union leadership to encourage women workers to see themselves as an important resource for the future of the American labor movement. Also see Barbara Wertheimer, "Search for a Partnership Role," in Jane Chapman, ed., *Economic Independence for Women* (Beverly Hills, London, Sage Publications, 1976).

E. Black and Other Minority Women

Amerasia Journal (Asian American Studies Center Publications, P.O. Box 24A43, Los Angeles, Calif., 90024). Entire issue devoted to problems confronting Asian women.

Bell, Carolyn, *The Economics of the Ghetto* (New York, Pegasus, 1970). Summarizes the problems confronting ghetto residents, including difficulties in obtaining employment.

The Black Scholar. Two special issues: "The Black Woman" (December 1971), contains essays on history and current situation of black women. "Black Women's Liberation" (March-April 1973) emphasizes the relationship between sexism and racism, including articles on the black male, sex stereotypes, and the black middle class.

Civil Rights Digest, vol. 6, no. 3 (Spring 1974) (U.S., Commission on Civil Rights). Excellent compilation of summary statements describing the problems confronting black and other minority women.

Commission on Civil Rights of Puerto Rico, *La Igualdad de Derechos y Oportunidades de Mujer Puertoriquena* (San Juan, 1972). A comprehensive survey of the position of women in Puerto Rican society, covering education, employment, economics, legal status, marriage, and the family, with recommendations for change. Includes biographies of noted women and a major bibliography.

Encore American and World Wide News, June 23, 1975, special issue on women. (515 Madison Avenue, New York).

Lerner, Gerda, ed., *Black Women in White America* (New York, Random House, 1972). A documentary history, including speeches, letters, poems, and essays covering slavery, education, racist sexism, work, achievements, and almost every other aspect of lives of black women in the United States. Lerner notes the double invisibility of black women and has, with this collection, done much to combat it.

Levitan, Sar A., William B. Johnston, and Robert Taggard, *Still a Dream: The Changing Status of Blacks Since 1960* (Cambridge, Harvard University Press, 1975). Summarizes data relating to social and economic status of blacks with chapters on black families and employment and earnings of black women compared to black men.

Longauex y Vasquez, Enriqueta, "The Mexican American Woman," in Robin Morgan, ed., *Sisterhood is Powerful* (New York, Random House, 1970). Examines the dilemmas of Chicanas as potential members of two movements: women's rights and the Chicano struggle, with particular attention to the plight of the Chicana as a single head of household.

Steiner, Stan, *The New Indians* (New York, Harper & Row, 1968). Chapter on "The Changing Woman," in particular, notes the important role of Indian women in much traditional life and in the current Native American movement.

U.S., Equal Employment Opportunity Commission, *Job Patterns for Minorities and Women in Private Industry, 1970* (Washington, D.C., Government Printing Office, 1972). This book is the result of a survey of 45,000 employers in private industry. Empirical data for the nation, each state, and selected metropolitan areas are provided on the number of females employed by particular industries.

———, *Negro Women in the Population and in the Labor Force* (Washington, D.C., Government Printing Office, 1967). Useful statistical data on the changing occupational patterns of black men and women, and the particular problems confronting black women up through the 1960s.

Ware, Cellestine, *Womanpower: The Movement for Women's Liberation* (New York, Tower Publications, Inc., 1970). An excellent account of the development of the women's movement in the late 1960s, together with an analysis of the relationship of black women to women's liberation.

II. Materials Related to Major Employment Categories of Women

A. *Clerical Workers*

Benet, Mary Kathleen, *The Secretarial Ghetto* (New York, McGraw Hill, 1972). Historical review of the rise of the secretary, emphasizing her position as the "office wife." Benet analyzes the way in which women are trained for these positions, the structures that keep them in their place, and the women's attitudes toward their situations.

Braverman, Harry, *Labor and Monopoly Capital* (New York,

London, Monthly Review Press, 1974). An inquiry into "the particular kinds of technological change characteristic of the monopoly capitalist period," which argues that this technology transformed work in a way that reduced the skills required of workers and thereby reduced them to performing relatively simple mechanical tasks. Examining this transformation in clerical work, Braverman links it to the growth of clerical functions, the increase in the number of workers, and mechanization and the introduction of "scientific management."

Coyle, Grace L., "Women in the Clerical Occupations," *The Annals of the American Academy of Political and Social Sciences,* 143: 80-187. This is an early article arguing that it is necessary to direct attention to the working conditions of clerical workers. It discusses the downgrading in the economic situation, status, and health of office workers as a result of changes in the technology of the office.

Davies, Margery, "Woman's Place Is at the Typewriter," *Radical America* 8 (July-August 1974): 1-28. An analytical account of the feminization of the clerical work force, this article relates the entry of women into the offices to shifts in the economy and the development of a new ideology that women "belong" in the office, in clerical positions.

Gooding, Judson, "The Fraying White Collar," *Fortune,* December, 1970. Gooding points out the irony in white collar jobs: although white collar workers are the mainstay of the business and service sectors of the economy, and these jobs are in large supply, the workers are becoming less secure. This is a good short article.

Lockwood, David, *The Blackcoated Worker* (London, 1958). This study analyzes the changing position of the clerk in British business and government. It focuses on male workers, but the analysis of the changes in the structure of the office, in the activities of the clerks, and in attitudes toward unionization are useful for understanding the female clerical labor force.

Mills, C. Wright, *White Collar* (New York, Oxford University Press, 1951). A sweeping sociological treatment of the work and workers necessitated by the social reorganization accompanying the rise of big business. Mills emphasizes the declining position of white collar workers in general and details the technical and organizational changes that are contributing to the development of dead-end jobs in clerical occupations.

Rico, Leonard, *The Advance Against Paperwork* (Ann Arbor,

Bureau of Industrial Relations, Graduate School of Business Administration, University of Michigan, 1967). The impact of computer systems on the organization of companies, on jobs, and on workers were surveyed in eighteen firms. In a chapter devoted to office work, Rico concludes that automation increases emphasis on formal routines, leads to finer subdivision of activities, and reduces the separation between the office and blue collar operations.

Rotella, Elyce, "Occupational Segregation and the Supply of Women to the American Clerical Labor Force, 1870-1930," presented at the Berkshire Conference on the History of Women, Radcliffe College, October 1974. This paper traces the rise in the supply of women clerical workers, arguing that women chose clerical work because it offered the best trade-off of wages relative to the training required among those occupations that were realistically open to women. Detailed statistical evidence.

Tepperman, Jean, *Not Servants, Not Machines* (Boston, Beacon Press, 1976). Using statistical information that traces the changing situation of office workers and interviews with office workers involved in the office workers movement, Tepperman provides an analysis of the office workers movement: its origins, its potential power and the obstacles it must overcome. The book connects the current movement to the historical changes in the nature of clerical work, to the present discontent, and to management strategies to prevent unionization, while offering suggestions for action based on the experience of the office workers movement. Wonderfully readable.

Waldman, Elizabeth, and B. McEaddy, "Where women work—an analysis by industry and occupation," *Monthly Labor Review* 97(5) (May 1974): 50-58. This article provides an overview of the trends in women's employment by industry and occupation. It notes that the phenomenal increase in the number and proportion of women (especially married women) joining the work force is the result of expansion in service industries that traditionally provide female jobs.

B. *Blue Collar Workers*

Chase, William H., *The American Woman, Her Changing Social, Economic and Political Roles 1920-1970* (New York, Oxford Press, 1972). Contains a summary and analysis of working women and their historical and present relation to trade unions in light of the social, economic, and political conditions.

First National Working Conference on Research: Women in Blue Collar Jobs (New York, Ford Foundation, December 1974). Brief summaries of thirty action and research projects dealing with blue collar working women. Proceedings and recommendations of the conference itself are not yet available.

Hedges, Janice, and Stephen Bemis, "Sex Stereotyping: Its Decline in Skilled Trades," *Monthly Labor Review* 97(5) (May 1974): 14-22. An optimistic account of the increase of women in skilled trades during the last ten years and their potential growth in the future with a discussion of the social, legal, and economic influencing factors.

Howe, I., ed., *The World of Blue Collar Workers* (New York, Quadrangle Books, 1972). A collection of articles reflecting several aspects of blue collar life. Two focus specifically on women and three on blacks. Myra Wolgong, vice president of the Hotel, Motel, and Restaurant Employees' Union talks about young women who work. Dorothy Rabinowitz focuses on the ILGWU, a predominantly female union with male leadership, and Judith Agassi on women who work in factories.

Komarovsky, Myra, *Blue Collar Marriage* (New York, Random House, 1964). Although dated, this is one of few studies that focuses on women in the working class and provides some useful insights into work and marriage among blue collar families.

O'Farrell, Brigid, "Affirmative Action for Women in Crafts: Change in the Small Industrial Work Group," paper presented at the SSP-American Sociological Association, Annual Meetings, 1975. Analysis of the impact of affirmative action in changing the status of women in nontraditional employment.

Roby, Pamela, *The Conditions of Women in Blue Collar, Industrial and Service Jobs: A Review of Research and Proposals for Research, Action and Policy* (New York, Russell Sage Foundation, 1974). Contains a review of the literature from 1890 to 1970, a summary of current research studies in woman power, women's liberation, unions and equal employment; and develops a research agenda in areas of wage and working conditions, work training and promotion opportunities, living conditions, policy affecting attitudes and unions. Also see Pamela Roby, "The Conditions of Women in Blue Collar Jobs," in Jane Chapman, ed., *Economic Independence for Women* (Beverly Hills, London, Sage Publications, 1976).

Seifer, Nancy, *Absent From the Majority: Working Class Women in*

America (New York, American Jewish Committee, Institute of Human Relations, 1973). Attempts to draw together the few existing studies and surveys of working class women, as well as first hand experiences of community leaders, organizers and observers to provide an impressionistic overview of the ways in which working class women's lives are beginning to change and the range of largely unexplored concerns which they face.

Sennet, Richard, and Jonathan Cobb, *The Hidden Injuries of Class,* (New York, Random House, 1972). An analysis of working class men in the Boston area, based on participant observation and 150 in-depth interviews with the men and their families. While women are specifically excluded, the book provides some useful insights into the attitudes of men that affect their response to women moving into the male blue collar jobs.

Stellman, Jeanne, and Susan Daum, *Work is Dangerous to Your Health: A Handbook of Health Hazards in the Workplace and What You Can Do About Them* (New York, Pantheon, 1973). While concerned with the occupational health and safety problems of all workers, the authors specifically call for research in the almost unexplored area of work related health problems for women, particularly in blue collar jobs.

Terkel, Studs, *Working* (New York, Pantheon Books, 1972). A series of interviews in a wide variety of occupations. While women are shown in traditional female jobs, several of the sections provide good descriptions of women who are investigating nontraditional blue collar jobs and how men feel about the jobs we are talking about moving women into.

C. *Service Workers*

(Note: Very little has been written about service workers per se. The following materials are primarily on related topics that would be useful in understanding women in service work. It is to be hoped that more directly relevant materials will soon be prepared.)

1. The Private Household Worker

Brecher, Charles, *Upgrading Blue Collar and Service Workers* (Baltimore, Johns Hopkins University Press, 1970).

"Eight Experimental and Demonstration Projects in the Household Employment," *Time Magazine,* April 5, 1968.

Massachusetts General Laws, Chapter 760, "An Act Making Domestic Employees Subject to the Labor Laws," August 24, 1970.

National Committee on Household Employment, "There Must Be A Code of Standards" and "Who are We?" (7705 George Ave., NW, Washington, D.C., 20802, 1974).

Parrish, Dorothy T., "Report of the Immigrant Domestic Program" (Boston, The Women's Service Club, Inc., 1966).

Porter, Sylvia, "Household Workers A Challenge To Change," *Mc-Call's Magazine*, October 1968.

Schlick, Mary D., and Ethlyn Christensen, "Household Employment," reprinted from *Word Magazine*, February 1969 (Washington, D.C., National Council of Women Publishers).

U.S., Department of Labor, Women's Bureau, "Consultation on the Status of Household Employment" (Washington, D.C., Government Printing Office, 1967). Report of the meeting, which examined ways of developing new concepts of household employment, fair wages, working conditions, performance standards. Emphasis was put on the employees' need for greater professionalism and rewards and the employers' need for more competent and better organized services.

U.S., Department of Labor, Employment Standards Administration, "Report of Consultation on Businesses in Household Employment and Follow Up Survey of Participating Firms" (Washington, D.C., Government Printing Office, 1970).

2. Background Materials for Women in Service Work

Levitan, Sar, D. Marwick, and M. Rein, *Work and Welfare Go Together* (Baltimore, Johns Hopkins University Press, 1972).

"Report to the Governor of Massachusetts from the Council on Public Employment of the Disadvantaged," Massachusetts Purchasing Agent No. 5895A, August 1971.

Resnicoff, Samuel, *Securing and Protecting Your Rights in Civil Service* (New York, Arco Publishing Press, 1973).

U.S., Office of Equal Opportunity, "Job Patterns for Minorities and Women in Private Industry," vol. 2, New England (Washington, D.C., Government Printing Office, 1973).

D. *Professional Workers*

Astin, Helen, *The Woman Doctorate in America: Origins, Careers and Family* (New York, Russell Sage Foundation, 1969). Well-documented survey of 1,653 women. Findings are used as basis for action proposals and future research possibilities. Includes nine autobiographical sketches.

Aufenkamp, Jane, "The Current Extent of Participation of Women in the Sciences," progress report, Federation of Organizations for Professional Women, January 20, 1975. Study concentrates on comparative data on men and women. Included is an excellent, while not annotated, bibliography on the field. Definition of sciences includes social science as well as engineering.

Blitz, Rudolph C., "Women in the Professions, 1870-1970," *Monthly Labor Review* 97(5) (May 1974): 34-39. Very useful historical analysis of women in the professions. Develops two indices: sex ratio (percent of women in a field) and occupational structure index (highlights declining and rising professions).

Carnegie Commission on Higher Education, *Opportunities for Women in Higher Eduation: Their Current Participation, Prospects for the Future, and Recommendations for Action* (New York, McGraw Hill, 1973). Description of the continuing trends of increased participation of women in graduate studies and teaching.

Committee on the College Student Group for the Advancement of Psychiatry, *The Educated Women: Prospects and Problems* 9(92) (January 1975). Psychological background material.

Eyde, Lorraine D., "Flexibility Through Part-time Employment of Career Workers in the Public Service," The Special Service Commission, June 1975. Study of part-time schedules in the public sector and recommendations for fitting part-time employment into the personnel ceiling system.

Kahne, Hilda, "The Women in Professional Occupations: New Complexities for Chosen Roles," *Journal of the National Association for Women Deans, Administrators, and Counselors,* vol. 39, no. 4 (Summer 1976). Covers employment outlook, work and the family, and flexible work structures.

Kundsin, Ruth B., ed., *Successful Women in the Sciences: An Analysis of the Determinants,* Annals of the New York Academy of Sciences, 208, March 1973. Very worthwhile collection of articles covering personal, educational, and economic facets of women in science. Twelve autobiographies by women in the field are also included.

Lopate, Carol, *Women in Medicine* (Baltimore, Johns Hopkins Press, 1968). Studies in-depth problems faced by female physicians both professionally and personally. Specific recommendations for increasing the number of qualified physicians are included.

Theodore, Athena, ed., *The Professional Woman* (Cambridge, Schenkman Publishing Co., 1971). Excellent collection of

articles, with an equally excellent bibliography of sources. Many
articles deal with specific professional occupations, for example,
doctors, librarians.

"Women in the Professions: What's All the Fuss About?" *American
Behavioral Scientist* 15 (November-December 1971). Entire
issue devoted to women in the professions; includes focus on
childhood socialization.

E. *Managers and Administrators*

Collegiate Woman's Career Magazine (Centerport, New York, Equal
Opportunity Publications). This new semi-annual periodical attempts to serve as a link between industry and college women
seeking employment. The most valuable section is the Corporate
Profile Directory that lists companies interested in recruiting
women and particular job opportunities available in the current
year.

Dunlap, Jan, *Personal and Professional Success for Women* (New
Jersey, Prentice Hall, 1972). How to cope with the frustrations
encountered in the workplace and derive positive elements from
failure or setback. The author emphasizes correct motivation
and development of attitudes and values that will bring success
on the job.

Killian, R. A., *The Working Woman: A Male Manager's View* (New
York, American Management Association, 1971). The author
presents a realistic view of problems experienced by women in
industry, based on many years as personnel director for a company that employs 15,000 women. However, this book is really
directed at the male manager having responsibilities for hiring
and developing employees.

Korda, M., *Male Chauvinism: How It Works* (New York, Random
House, 1973). Examines the problems arising from the subordi-
nation of women in the office environment and speculates on
why male chauvinism exists. The book contains mostly anec-
dotes and vignettes.

Loring, R., and Theodora Wells, *Breakthrough: Women Into Management* (New York, Van Nostrand, Reinhold, 1972).

ORC Public Opinion Index, "Bias at the Top: Attitudes of the Nation's Executives Toward the Management Potential of Women
and Minorities" (Princeton, Opinion Research Corporation,
July 1974).

Pogrebin, Letty Cottin, *How to Make it in a Man's World* (New
York, Doubleday, 1970). This book was written by a woman

who has had an exciting career as publicity director for the publisher, Bernard Geis. Chatty and humorous at times, it provides entertainment as well as good tips on "making it in a man's world" on a day-to-day basis.

Ralston, Mary, *How to Return to Work in an Office* (New York, Harper & Row, 1973). Practical advice from a woman with twenty years of experience in personnel work on obtaining and sharpening marketable skills, presenting a professional appearance, preparing a resume, selecting a child care center, and so on; written especially for the person who has been away from the working world for a number of years.

"Women in Management: Pattern for Change," *Harvard Business Review*, July-August 1971. Article in which authors urge corporate leaders to respond positively to pressures for equal opportunities for women. Article describes four-step program for the organization that wants to take initiative in employing more women managers. Program includes making occupational census, gathering data on former employees, revisiting recruiting procedures, and expanding training opportunities for women.

III. General Annotated Bibliographies Relating to Women

Astin, Helen, Allison Parelman, and Ann Fisher, *Sex Roles: A Research Bibliography* (Washington, Center for Human Services, 1975). Over 450 extensively annotated entries arranged in topical fashion for easy reference.

Bickner, Mei Liang, *Women at Work: An Annotated Bibliography* (Los Angeles, Institute of Industrial Relations, University of California, 1974). A bibliography including more than 600 entries with author, title, category, and key word index.

Davis, Lenwood G., *The Black Woman in American Society* (Boston, G. K. Hall & Co., 1975). Annotated bibliography including some 700 books, articles, reports, documents, pamphlets. The subject index is limited.

Healy, Regina, and Diane Lund, *Chapter 622: Massachusetts Law, Women and Vocational Education*, prepared for the National Institute of Education (Boston, Organization of Social and Technical Innovation [OSTI], 1975). Provides a valuable bibliography relating to vocational education and women.

Kahne, Hilda, "Economic Perspectives on the Roles of Women in the American Economy," *Journal of Economic Literature*, December 1975. Provides a review of the economic literature that specifically addresses women, both in the home and at work, or that provides a framework for analysis of women. Included are over 250 references.

Kohen, Andrew I., Susan C. Breinich, and Patricia Shields, *Women and the Economy: A Bibliography and a Review of the Literature on Sex Differentiation in the Labor Market* (Center for Human Resource Research, College of Administrative Science, Ohio State University, March 1975). While entries are not annotated, the citations are organized according to a topical outline containing twenty-seven categories and subcategories, particularly useful for occupational research.

Rosenberg, Marie Barovic, and Len V. Bergstrom, *Women and Society: A Critical Review of the Literature with a Selected Annotated Bibliography* (New York, Sage Publications, 1975). An extensive listing of 3,600 annotated entries. The inclusion of an addendum is helpful by updating through February 1974.

Workshop Participants

Workshop I. On Women (Re)entering the Paid Labor Force

Co-Conveners: Patricia Mittenthal, Carol Ryser

Sandra Budson, Continuum
Brandeis University*
Waltham, MA

Anne Buschine
Wellesley, MA

Sondra Darling and Alice
    Dunwoody
Women's Inner City Educational
    Resource Service
Roxbury, MA

Kathy Day, Manpower
    Administration
U.S. Dept. of Labor—Room
    1600
Boston, MA

Ernestine Garcia
Hartford, CT

Claire Goulette
People for Welfare Justice and
    Council on Higher Education
Manchester, NH

Lila Hexner
Women's Opportunity Research
    Center
Middlesex Community College
Bedford, MA

Elaine Holmstrom
Women's Resource Center
Framingham, MA

Marilyn Huntington
Holliston, MA

Jan Nannen, Margaret Link
Trinity-Rensselaer Institute for
    Community Education
Hartford, CT

*Organizational affiliations are listed for purposes of identification only.

Jean McGuire, Metropolitan
    Council for Educational
    Opportunity
Roxbury, MA

Joyce Slayton Mitchell
Consultant in Education
Wolcott, VT

Marjorie O'Byrne
Women in Communication
Newton, MA

Carol Pierce
New Dynamics Associates
Laconia, NH

Anne Pomroy
Governor's Council on the
    Status of Women
Augusta, ME

Paula Ann Ross
Boston, MA

Marjorie Schiller
Office of the Senate
Boston, MA

Deborah Stoessel
Widening Horizons for Women
Concord, MA

Kate Villers, New Communities
Boston, MA

Dottie Watron, Personnel
    Department
Polaroid Corporation
Waltham, MA

Barbara L. Wilson, Career
    Services
Wellesley College
Wellesley, MA

Evelyn Zuk, Adult Education
Concord Public Schools
Concord, MA

Workshop II. On Black and Other Minority Women

Convener: Ramona Hoage Edelin
Research Assistant: Debra Attiya Melton

Jewel Chambers
U.S. Office of Education
Boston, MA

Freda Garcia
Consultation and Education
Boston, MA

Mary Goode
State House of Representatives,
    Massachusetts
Roxbury, MA

Jacquelyne Jackson*
Duke University Medical Center
Durham, NC

Susan Lincoln
South Central Community
    College
New Haven, CT

*Absent Sunday and, therefore, did not participate in final definition.

Rosalind Matthews
Director of Career Opportunities,
    Textron
Providence, RI

Eunice Mabray
Providence, RI

Phyllis McGrane
Old Town, ME

Ruth Moy*
Chinese Golden Age Center
Boston, MA

Diann Painter
Department of Economics
Wellesley College
Wellesley, MA

Helen Stewart
Cambridge, MA

Ernestina Walcott
Mattapan, MA

*Absent Sunday and, therefore, did not participate in final definition.

Workshop III. On Clerical Workers

Co-conveners: Roslyn Feldberg, Evelyn Glenn
Research Assistant: Irma Claxton Scruggs

Ann Alach
Harvard Medical School
Canton, MA

Anne Boudreau, Representative
Maine State Legislature
Portland, ME

Linda Carr
Travelers Insurance Company
Manchester, CT

Sally Connolly
Skill Center
New Haven, CT

Judy McCullough
9 to 5
Boston, MA

Elinor Menez
Women's Task Force
U.S. Dept. of Transportation
Cambridge, MA

Margaret Murray
The Governor's Commission
    on the Status of Women
Montpelier, VT

Sandy Nelson
International Union
    Representative
AFSCME
South Barre, VT

Mellanee Newkirk
Small Business Administration
Roxbury, MA

Vermelle Parks
Boston Manpower
    Administration
Boston, MA

Dorothy Parrish
Massachusetts Commission
    Against Discrimination
Boston, MA

Janet Reagan
Office of Federal Contract
    Compliance
Boston, MA

Josephine Steckevicz
Cooperative Business Program
Merrimack High School
Merrimack, NH

Leslie Sullivan
District 65, D.W.A.
Boston, MA

Jean Tepperman
Dorchester, MA

Alice Wilkins
Augusta, ME

Programs Panel

Pat Harvey, Vice President
Boston University
Boston, MA

Joanne Keenan
Director of Field
    Administration
John Hancock Mutual Life
    Insurance Company
Boston, MA

George White, Equal
    Employment Officer
U.S. Civil Service
    Commission
Boston, MA

Workshop IV. On Service Workers

Convener: Dorothy T. Parrish
Research Assistant: Julianne Malveaux

Royal L. Bolling, Jr.
Massachusetts State Legislature
Boston, MA

Major Fowler
Roxbury, MA

Alice Freeman
The Project Director
Women's Service Club
Boston, MA

Dorothy Garrison, Director
Family and Community
   Services
Action for Boston Community
   Development
Boston, MA

Virginia Lee
Roxbury, MA

John Martin, Chairman
Industrial Accident Board
Boston, MA

Yvonne Matthews
Hyde Park, MA

Barbara McLean
Women's Service Club
Boston, MA

Margaret Murray
The Governor's Commission
   on the Status of Women
Montpelier, VT

Aida Nesselroth, Coordinator
Family Life Course—
   Windham High School
Storrs, CT

Saul Nesselroth
Labor Education Center,
   University of Connecticut
Storrs, CT

Roxie Parker, Unit Manager
Peter Bent Brigham Hospital
Mattapan, MA

Ed Simone
Room 520
Boston, MA

Edith B. Sloan,
   Executive Director
National Committee on
   Household Employment
Washington, DC

Workshop V. On Blue Collar Workers

Convener: Brigid O'Farrell
Research Assistant: Marianne Ajenian

Ruth Benjamin
Recruitment and Training Program
Mattapan, MA

Hedy Ferrera
Int'l Ladies Garment
   Workers Union
Fairhaven, MA

Karen Fischer
Bureau of Labor Education
University of Maine
Orono, ME

Jane Kelly
House of Representatives
Hampton, NH

Barbara Lewis
International Union
    Electrical Workers
Lynnfield, MA

Mary Miller
Equal Employment
    Opportunity Commission
Boston, MA

Anne Nelson
Women's Trade Union Program
Cornell University
New York, NY

Vermelle Parks
Boston Manpower
    Administration
Boston, MA

Eva Sartwell, V.P.
State AFL-CIO
Concord, NH

Betty Tianti
Committee on
    Political Education
State Labor Council,
    AFL-CIO
Hamden, CT

Grace Walker
Concord Credit Union
Concord, NH

Employer Panel

Karen Govan
EEO Staff
Boston Edison Power
    & Light Co.
Boston, MA

Elly Perisi
EEO Staff
Sears Robuck Co.
Natick, MA

R. F. Spousta
Apprenticeship Training
General Electric Co.
Lynn, MA

Palmer True
Production Department
Polaroid Corporation
Waltham, MA

Workshop VI. On Professional Workers

Convener: Hilda Kahne
Research Assistant: Diane Hurley

Rhoda Baruch
Director, Career Development
    Office
Dartmouth College
Hanover, NH

Janet Brown
President, Federation of
    Organizations for
    Professional Women
Washington, DC

Arlene Kaplan Daniels
Director, The Project on Women
Northwestern University
Evanston, IL

Faith Dunne
Department of Education
Dartmouth College
Hanover, NH

Lilli Hornig, Director
Higher Education Resources
   Service
Brown University
Providence, RI

Rosabeth Kanter
Department of Sociology
Brandeis University
Waltham, MA

Herta Loeser, Director
Civic Center and
   Clearing House
Boston, MA

Rosalind Matthews
Director of Career Opportunity
Textron
Providence, RI

Gene Ott, Director
Computer Science
Wellesley College
Wellesley, MA

Diann Painter
Economics Department
Wellesley College
Wellesley, MA

Marjorie Schiller, Special Asst.
Office of the Senate President
State House
Boston, MA

Sally Seymour, Asst. Director
Regional Institute on
   Employment, Training and
   Labor Market Policy
Boston University
Boston, MA

Ruth G. Shaeffer
Senior Research Associate
Organization Development
National Industrial
   Conference Board
New York, NY

Eleanore Silverman
Registrar
Wellesley College
Wellesley, MA

Nancy Watts, Assistant Director
Educational Planning for
   Curriculum Development
The Massachusetts General
   Hospital
Boston, MA

Barbara Lazarus Wilson
Director, Career Services
Wellesley College
Wellesley, MA

Robert W. Eisenmenger
Senior Vice President and
   Director of Research
Federal Reserve Bank
Boston, MA

Workshop VII. On Managerial and Administrative Workers

Convener: Doris Mitchell
Research Assistant: Erline Willis

Vivian Buckles
Regional Director of Women's
   Bureau
U.S. Department of Labor
Boston, MA

Catherine Davidson
Assoc. Director of Government
   Affairs and Law Division
Cash and Property Department
Travelers Insurance Company
Hartford, CT

Grace Flores, Program Specialist
Office of the Secretary
Planning and Evaluation
HEW, Room 3522
Washington, DC

Susan Green
Management Program Developer
Grad. Programs in Management
West Newton, MA

Judi Hampton
Director of Consumer Affairs
Mobil Oil Corportaion
Washington, DC

Carol A. Hannaford
Assistant Vice President
Cambridge Savings Bank
Cambridge, MA

Barbara Jackson
Associate Dean, Atlanta
   University
School of Education
Director of Ph.D. Program in
   Ed. Admin.
Atlanta, GA

Evelyn Murphy
Secretary of Environmental
   Affairs
Commonwealth of
   Massachusetts
Boston, MA

Kathie Nicholson
Manager Personnel Policy
   & Planning
Star Market Company
Cambridge, MA

Glendora Putnam
Deputy Assistant Secretary
   for Fair Housing and
   Equal Opportunity
Washington, DC

Miriam Meyers Ritvo
Dean of Students
Lesley College
Cambridge, MA

Jayne Soles
Manager of Graphic Quality
South Windham, ME

Elaine Selle
Director, Publishing Division
Dartmouth Printing Company
Hanover, NH

Workshop VIII. On A Strategy for Education

Convener: Joan Wofford

Deborah Ashford
Staff Assistant, Women's
  Affairs
Bureau of Occupational
  and Adult Education
U.S. Office of Education
Washington, DC

Cynthia A. Beaudoin
LaSalle Junior College
Brookline, MA

Muriel Cohen
Educational Editor
Boston Globe
Dorchester, MA

Patricia Fritts,
  Consultant
Barnstable, MA

Roland Goddu, Director
New England Program for
  Teacher Education
Durham, NH

Henry Morgan
School of Management
Boston University
Boston, MA

Miriam Myers Ritvo
Dean of Students
Lesley College
Cambridge, MA

Herbert R. Waters, Jr.
Principal, Carnegie Academy/
  County Street School
  Complex
North Dartmouth, MA

Index

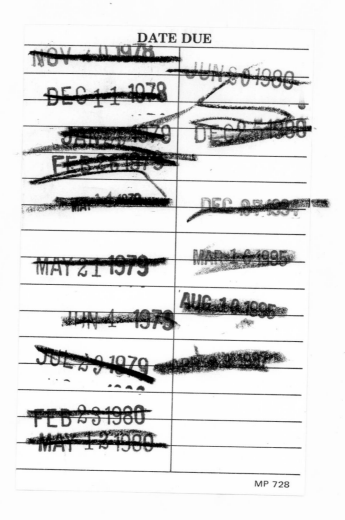

DATE DUE

NOV ~~1978~~	JUN ~~30 1980~~
DEC ~~1 1 1978~~	
~~JAN 1979~~	DEC ~~1980~~
FEB ~~26 1979~~	
~~MAY~~	DEC ~~05 1991~~
MAY ~~21 1979~~	MAR ~~16 1995~~
JUN ~~1 1979~~	AUG ~~10 1995~~
JUL ~~29 1979~~	
FEB ~~23 1980~~	
MAY ~~12 1980~~	

MP 728